Advance Praise

"Our team at Morning Brew enjoyed some laughs with a virtual scavenger hunt led by Kristi's team at JAM, and we fully agree with the ideas shared in her book. Playing and laughing together will strengthen bonds among your team, enhancing creativity and innovation no matter what industry you're in."

—**ALEX LIEBERMAN**, Co-Founder and
Executive Chairman of Morning Brew

"It Pays to PLAY is spot on. Great leadership means understanding how to create engagement with your team, and Kristi Herold has definitely mastered this! A must-read for anyone interested in understanding and implementing the power of play."

—**KARA GOLDIN**, Founder of Hint Inc. and
author of the WSJ bestseller Undaunted

"Having known Kristi for over twenty years, I can confidently say no one knows the power of play better, and when it comes to injecting fun and play in the workplace, she is worth listening to."

—**BRIAN SCUDAMORE**, Founder and CEO of
1-800-GOT-JUNK? and O2E Brands

"Kristi Herold shares the secret that many great leaders have known for years: teams that play together, stay together."

—**ROBERT GLAZER**, WSJ and *USA Today* bestselling author of *Elevate*, *Friday Forward*, and *How to Thrive in the Virtual Workplace*

"There's no one in the world who understands the importance of play in the workplace better than Kristi Herold. With It Pays To PLAY, she shares the secret to building a great company culture and happy customers. This is the book that I wish I had when I started in the industry."

—**JESSE COLE**, owner of the Savannah Bananas and author of *Fans First*

"Kristi Herold's collection of real-life stories and studies about the importance of play for physical and mental health, combined with tactical ideas on implementation, provide the motivation you need to improve your corporate culture for the betterment of your entire team."

—**BEN GREENFIELD**, human performance consultant, speaker, and NYT bestselling author of seventeen books, including *Beyond Training*, *Boundless*, and *Fit Soul*

"This book isn't a steamy romance novel. But it will get your heart racing, your face smiling, and your body moving in ways you never thought possible. Don't press play. Read about it. Then do it, and get your team doing it too."

—**RON TITE**, author of *Think. Do. Say.*

"Kristi Herold is a groundbreaking changemaker in understanding the power of play and creating an engaged and energized workplace. We are lucky she is so generous to share her insights and innovations that you can apply immediately to your organization. Play becomes profitable through the learnings in her book."

—**MARK HARRISON**, Founder of MH3 Collective

"Kristi Herold's book It Pays to PLAY is a vital leadership resource that will help all business leaders as they seek to create fun corporate cultures that clearly show their employees they care about stress reduction, improved physical and mental health, and team bonding."

—**JJ VIRGIN**, celebrity nutrition and fitness expert and NYT bestselling author

"This is a must-read book for anyone looking to improve their business culture. Play in the workplace is often overlooked, and as Kristi Herold shares and our team at G Adventures has experienced, play has the power to improve loyalty, engagement and creativity."

—**BRUCE POON TIP**, Founder of G Adventures

"In an outcome-focused world that's stressed out, we've lost the power of play. This book gives you the roadmap to transform your culture and your bottom line."

—**TODD HERMAN**, author of The Alter Ego Effect

"Play is a powerful method to connect teams. Kristi Herold outlines how to play in a way that's engaging, inspiring, and not the least bit cheesy."

—**DAVID BURKUS**, author of *Leading from Anywhere*

"While our Franklin Sports team knows a lot about playing sports and sports equipment, we have made the choice to invest in Kristi and her team at JAM to help us connect through play on multiple occasions. As her book suggests, investing in play at work will pay for itself."

—**ADAM FRANKLIN**, President, Franklin Sports

IT PAYS TO
PLAY

IT PAYS TO
PLAY

HOW PLAY
IMPROVES
BUSINESS
CULTURE

KRISTI HEROLD

LIONCREST
PUBLISHING

It Pays to PLAY

How Play Improves Business Culture

ISBN 978-1-5445-3621-7 Hardcover

978-1-5445-3622-4 Paperback

978-1-5445-3623-1 Ebook

To my three children, Cassidy, Andie, and Dax,
as well as my three bonus-children, Nicholas, Georgia, and Iain:
whether we are playing a card game, going on hikes,
throwing a disc, or playing guitar and singing,
I thank you for indulging my love of PLAY.

To DB, my seventh child, oldest in age yet youngest in spirit,
thank you for filling my days with love and laughter.

And to my father, John Herold, who passed away
just weeks before this book was going to print.
Dad loved to PLAY, and he was my earliest mentor and
entrepreneurial inspiration. He taught me the
importance of caring about culture and our people.
While Dad was not an avid reader, I know he would have
read this book and told everyone he knew about it,
as he was always my biggest fan and support.
Keep playing Dad—I love you.

CONTENTS

Introduction. 1

CHAPTER 1 15
PLAY Improves Retention

CHAPTER 2 47
PLAY Increases Engagement

CHAPTER 3 83
PLAY Improves Health

CHAPTER 4 127
PLAY Improves Energy

CHAPTER 5 157
PLAY Increases Creativity

CHAPTER 6 187
PLAY Creates Happier Customers

Conclusion 211

So Why PLAY?

Appendix 215

Ideas for PLAY at Work

Acknowledgments 237

About the Author 243

INTRODUCTION

*"It is utterly false and cruelly arbitrary
to put all the play and learning into childhood,
all the work into middle age, and
all the regrets into old age."*

—MARGARET MEAD

Play is powerful. It has stopped war in its tracks!

Just look at the Olympic competitions and festivals held in ancient Greece. During the Persian and Peloponnesian wars, truces were made, and fighting was suspended. Armies were not allowed to threaten the games or the visitors traveling to attend them. Legal disputes were forbidden while the Olympic contests were being held, and there was a moratorium on capital punishment.

This arrangement was known as the "Olympic Truce," and to make sure everyone honored it, an inscription explaining the accord was put on a bronze discus and displayed for all to see.

> The ancient Greeks valued the art of playing games so much that it took precedence over fighting, leading them to take the remarkable step of suspending all war maneuvers, legal squabbles, army attacks, and death sentences until playtime was over.

Fast forward more than two millennia to World War I, and there are accounts of how the powerful impact of play was able to stop war in its tracks yet again.

In December of 1914, German and Allied troops were actively engaged in war. But as Christmas approached, something changed. For one day, in what would go down in history as the "Christmas Truce," the soldiers put down their guns, crossed battle lines, and *played* together. A widespread, unofficial cease-fire took hold along the whole Western Front, with enemy soldiers coming together to exchange greetings and play impromptu games of soccer (or football, as it's called in most of the world).

Christmas Truce

Men who had literally been shooting each other hours earlier stopped everything to play a game, kicking a ball around the battlefields. The power of play was so strong that it literally stopped the war, at least temporarily, and even bridged linguistic barriers to bring opposing sides together for a few welcome moments of lighthearted fun and social interaction.

If play is powerful enough to stop war, imagine how powerfully it can positively impact your workplace!

PLAY: A Definition

Verb: engage in activity for enjoyment and recreation rather than a serious or practical purpose.

Many businesspeople hold the staunch belief that play does not belong at work, thinking instead that work is work, play is play, and never the two shall mix.

Yet, Margaret Mead, a daring independent woman who was not afraid to explore and discuss taboo or challenging topics, and who has been a model for all those willing to learn and challenge the status quo, is known for having said, "It is utterly false and cruelly arbitrary to put all the play and learning into childhood, all the work into middle age, and all the regrets into old age."

I am apt to agree with Ms. Mead on this. I believe that the benefits of play are so incredibly powerful that it is critical for strong business leaders to make time for it in the workplace. And I believe that in doing so, you will see improvements in retention, engagement, physical and mental health, energy, creativity, and customer satisfaction.

PLAY Is a Natural State

Birds do it, bees do it, even educated fleas do it. Dogs do it, dolphins do it, and every one of us as children did it too. I'm not talking about sex; I'm talking about play! Across species, we observe playful behavior as a natural state. In the wild, lions wrestle with each other and even play an animal version of hide-and-seek. In dog parks, canines of all sizes (who've never even met before) engage in excited playtime, tackling each other, vulnerably showing their underbellies, and running around wagging their tails wildly. Then, of course, there is our own species: kids *love* to play—at school, home, or wherever they may be. For children, play is a biological drive and the primary mechanism through which they encounter and explore their immediate physical environments. Children play instinctively with natural elements and can turn pretty much anything into a game.

The fact is, play is both natural and powerful. It provides an energy boost, engages the imagination, and helps to develop problem-solving skills. Certainly, play is prevalent in the lives of most children. But now we also know that individuals who are fortunate enough to *keep* a playful attitude as adults are likely to benefit in many ways.

Through this book, we will see how play can help busy adults by the following:

- Reducing their stress levels

- Increasing creativity

- Creating stronger relationships

- Boosting their energy levels

- Keeping their minds sharp

- Improving their mental and physical health

- Staying happier in general

PLAY in the Workplace Pays Big Dividends

Workplace wellness has become a hot topic in the business world, which is fantastic. It is so important that as leaders we take a holistic approach and consider the overall well-being of our employees. Having said that, most organizations currently seem to be focused on things like health benefits, healthy snacks, gym memberships, meditation practices—all individually focused items. Very little focus has been placed on social connections among work teams, the uniquely created bonds and friendships that form within communities when we play together.

This book is dedicated to showing leaders—in businesses of all sizes, everywhere—that play in the workplace is an essential part of a healthy corporate culture. Simply put, an investment in play leads to *happier, more productive employees, a stronger organizational culture, and greater profits.*

In the following chapters, you'll find out why employees stick around longer in a more playful work environment and how encouraging play in your business can boost engagement, creativity, productivity, and profitability, as well as help improve the mental and physical health of your team. Not only will your employees benefit, but your customers will be happier. Your bottom line will be healthier too...something *every* business owner and manager strives for. You will also be provided with ideas and resources for a multitude of easy-to-implement ways to incorporate play at work, something that needn't be complicated, costly, or time-consuming. In reading this book, I trust you will recognize and come to agree that it really does pay to play.

By the end of the book, you'll see that making time for play is just as important as other facets of your business, like hiring, marketing, or production, and can make your organization stronger than you ever imagined.

Are Your Employees Having Fun?

To some, this may seem an odd question. After all, you hire your employees to work, not to have fun, right?

Wrong. Of course, you have hired your staff to work and serve your organization through their efforts. But if they're not having fun, making meaningful connections, and enjoying what they're doing throughout the hours they work each day (especially given we typically spend 35 percent of our total waking hours at work[1]), odds are they are not going to stick around long.

Look no further than the much-discussed trend known as The Great Resignation, which affected all industries in the wake of the COVID-19 pandemic of 2020 and 2021. In 2021, workers started leaving their jobs at historic rates. This sudden exodus occurred for a variety of reasons, including rampant stress, the shift to remote work—and a search for better pay, more meaningful purpose, and improved work culture and conditions.

---

[1] Karl Thompson, "What Percentage of Your Life Will You Spend at Work?" Revise Sociology, August 16, 2016, https://revisesociology.com /2016/08/16/percentage-life-work/.

Many organizations have struggled to address the problem and will continue to struggle if they don't understand why their employees are leaving in the first place. Rather than take the time to investigate the true causes of attrition, many companies are jumping to well-intentioned quick fixes like bumping up pay or offering "thank you" bonuses without making an effort to strengthen the relationships among their teams. What often ends up happening with this approach is that employees sense a transaction, and transactional relationships tend to breed resentment, not loyalty.

According to a data-driven study reported on by MIT Sloan Management Review,[2] the biggest predictor of employee resignations was a toxic culture. The report went on to say that "a toxic corporate culture is by far the strongest predictor of industry-adjusted attrition and is ten times more important than compensation in predicting turnover."

---

[2] Donald Sull, Charles Sull, and Ben Zweig, "Toxic Culture Is Driving the Great Resignation," MIT Sloan Management Review, January 11, 2022, https://sloanreview.mit.edu/article/toxic-culture-is-driving-the-great -resignation/.

Building a Great Culture

Having the type of work culture that other business leaders envy and want to emulate doesn't happen by accident; it takes intention and a commitment to the well-being of your individual employees and the overall team.

In 1996, I founded (and for the last twenty-five years have led) a B2C company called the Sport & Social Group (SSG) that connected people through playing in adult recreational sports leagues. It started with a few hundred players in Toronto and has grown to be one of the largest organizations of its kind in the world, with hundreds of thousands of people playing annually across thirteen cities (and many more in the works!). During that time, we also gained recognition for building a great and fun organizational culture. As a result, I am often asked to speak on company culture to a variety of business groups around North America.

During the pandemic, employees lost their watercooler moments, their lunches with office pals, and their afterwork corporate sports teams or drinks with colleagues. They lost their human connection with their peers—and this loss was a hit to workplace cultures around the globe. At SSG, our sports leagues were also shut down, so my own tight-knit team found ourselves not only dealing with the low morale we all felt suddenly working from home, but also the shock of having our twenty-five-year-old business shut down due to government mandates.

We knew we wanted to stay true to our core purpose of connecting people through play. And, of course, we needed to find a way for our organization to survive. So we pivoted to creating a B2B service that offered hosted virtual events, helping corporate teams around the world stay connected through play. This shift helped boost the morale of my own team as well as the morale of the thousands of company teams we helped connect through play globally.

After this massive pivot, we also decided to rebrand our organization from the Sport & Social Group to JAM. We are now providing even more diverse ways for people to connect through play and for companies to improve profits through play, by offering everything from recreational sports leagues to virtual escape rooms or game shows to in-person corporate field days and scavenger hunts. Everything we do at JAM revolves around the strengthening of human connections and corporate cultures by playing together.

I have spent the last twenty-six years connecting people through play and working to have a strong culture in my own business. Now it's time to share my insights on the powerful benefits of play in the workplace. Whatever type of business you're in, and whatever the size of your organization, you'll see by the end of this book why you must make time for play.

In a changing business landscape where nothing is the same as it was, even just a few years ago, the choice is clear. Making time for play pays huge dividends, and you simply can't afford *not* to bring play into your workplace.

In the following chapters, you'll get a deeper look into why play is so important and how it can transform your business —but only *if* you start to take your employees' need to play seriously.

Some of what you may notice when you make room for play is this:

- Employee retention and loyalty will improve. They will stick around longer.

- Your organization will have a better overall vibe, which will be felt by your employees and customers alike. Your company's energy will feel better, and people will take notice!

- Employees will be healthier and happier and will perform better because they're having serious fun.

- Friendships and bonds will strengthen in the workplace, which will improve collaboration, creativity, communication, and teamwork.

When you make time for play and fun, everyone benefits, including you and your bottom line.

PLAY Improves Retention

"Choose a job you love, and you will never have to work a day in your life."

—CONFUCIUS

D id you know that the average cost of replacing an employee is 50–150 percent of their annual salary? [3]

---

[3] "Employee Retention—What is the True Cost of Losing an Employee?" Simply Benefits, July 25, 2020, https://www.simplybenefits.ca/blog /employee-retention-what-is-the-true-cost-of-losing-an-employee.

When somebody who's earning a salary of $50,000 a year leaves your business, it will cost you between $25,000 and $75,000 to fill that position with someone new.

I recently spoke with my friend Gerrard Schmid, former CEO of the multinational Diebold Nixdorf Corporation that has 26,000 employees. Their turnover was typically 8 percent annually, which meant hiring 2,000 new people every year. When the pandemic hit in 2020, and then the "Great Resignation" followed shortly after, they saw their turnover increase to 12 percent, creating a need for the recruiting, hiring, onboarding, and training of 3,000 new employees annually. According to Gerrard, this became a huge drain on their HR team and a huge financial burden to the organization. And as he aptly pointed out, clearly it makes financial sense to look for a variety of impactful ways to invest in the retention of your people.

Money isn't the only reason to work to retain your employees. Any time an employee leaves and a new person comes in, there's a period of adjustment and learning curves to ride. The company culture shifts to some degree as new personalities are introduced and team dynamics change. High turnover rates chip away at your workplace culture, creating instability and a creeping dissatisfaction that can torpedo all your well-intended efforts.

This isn't to suggest that all turnover is bad. Sometimes, like with crop rotation—the practice of planting different crops on the same plot of land to improve soil health and optimize nutrients in the soil—staff turnover and change can be beneficial. When we have teammates who have plateaued and/or if you have a bad apple in the bunch, bringing in fresh new recruits can provide a positive culture shift.

Suffice to say, given how costly high turnover is to an organization, managers and business leaders *have* to find better ways to reduce turnover as well as to attract and recruit new teammates more easily and effectively. Doing so makes both financial and cultural sense.

The Cost of High Turnover Rates

Why does it cost 50–150 percent of a person's salary to replace them?

These are the top reasons:

- *Time*: Weeks (or months) can go by before a qualified person is found to fill the vacancy.

- *Productivity*: When a key person leaves, productivity in that segment of the business can grind

to a halt. Coworkers have to take on more responsibilities to cover for the employee who has left,
leaving little time or energy for their own work.

- *Stress:* When your remaining staff are left to
  shoulder the workload for teammates who have
  resigned, this creates an additional burden on
  them, which will increase their stress as well as
  the risk of burnout among your team.

- *Recruiting:* Your HR people have to put aside
  whatever projects they're working on to instead
  focus on finding, attracting, and interviewing
  new candidates.

- *Onboarding:* It takes days to weeks to go through
  the process of bringing a new person on board
  and getting them prepped for the work ahead.

- *Training:* It takes weeks to months to fully train
  this person and get them up to speed.

If your organization is trying to grow and advance, losing
employees can seriously hurt your growth goals and impact
your schedule. And if it happens too frequently, you can begin
to feel like you are on a hamster wheel, focusing constantly
on rebuilding your team instead of growing your business.

Even if you're focused solely on your day-to-day business operations without thinking about growth, losing a key employee can set you back. The disruption can lead to issues like irate customers who are not getting what they need or missed production deadlines that can set you back a full quarter or longer.

What's more, there's an emotional cost to losing an employee that's hard to put a number on. It can be demoralizing and can impact your culture in a negative way. Others on your team may start to wonder, *Should I stay?* or *Should I start looking around for something better?* If you're not careful, you could wind up with a domino effect where, one by one, all your great employees start turning in their resignation letters.

My Personal Experience with the Pain of Turnover

When I was in university, I spent three summers running a College Pro Painters (CPP) franchise. CPP hired and trained university students on how to run residential painting businesses during their summers off from school. Even though I studied business in university, nothing I learned in the classroom came close to this real-world experience of running my own franchise. The training I received and the experiences I gained were better than any business degree.

I was immediately thrown into the deep end, responsible for marketing, sales, recruiting painters, hiring, training, scheduling, and production. It was a hands-on crash course with real money, real employees, and real customers all on the line.

That first summer, I had eight painters working for me, all of them also university students. I'd spent a lot of time interviewing, hiring, and training these painters; I'd also done all my marketing and had numerous jobs sold and ready to produce through May and June.

Toward the end of June however, four painters—half my team—quit on me. I had to stop everything. I couldn't do any more marketing or go out and sell jobs until I took care of replacing the painters who'd left.

This cost me tremendously. I lost production time. I lost marketing time. I lost selling time. Everything came to a screeching halt while I scrambled to recruit other painters and train these new hires.

The reason four of my painters left, frankly, was because I

was a horrible boss. I was acting like a dictator. I wasn't showing that I cared about these employees as people or treating them like teammates. I was focused only on the numbers for my business. I was entirely driven by getting jobs done on time and delivering a quality service to the customer, without taking the time to check in with my team of painters to see how they were doing personally or in their jobs.

I found out after this group of painters quit that one of them had a fear of heights which was holding him back. Had I taken time to check in with him, I would have heard his concerns, and I would have been able to schedule him on jobs that were lower and/or with other crew members who were keen to do the high-ladder work.

It didn't feel great to realize I had blown it. Not sure where else to turn, I sat down with my dad—a small business owner himself—to talk about the problems I had been experiencing running my painting franchise.

My dad was an entrepreneur through and through. While he did complete an undergraduate degree, we always joked that he was far more "street-smart" than "book-smart." Many of our family dinner conversations revolved around business, with both my parents always encouraging my brothers and me to work for what we wanted in life. The lifestyle my dad was able to create from his entrepreneurial endeavors—in terms of both financial freedom and the freedom to control his own time (he never missed a family dinner or cheering us on at our extracurricular events)—was inspirational for all of us. So naturally he was my first mentor in business.

When I went to my dad after my painters had quit, he shared a very important lesson with me: *people are priority.* They are the lifeblood of any organization. In fact, my dad believed that people are the most important part of a successful organization. He explained it like this: if you don't have great people who are happy to be working with you, then you're not going to be able to run a successful business. As I recall, what he bluntly said was "without good people, you've got nothing." Simple as that.

He was right, of course. I had been doing everything correctly *except* for the most important piece, which was treating my *people* well, and this had derailed my business' success. Thankfully, I took the setback as an opportunity and changed my focus.

From that point forward, I revised the way I ran my organization, with a focus on people as priority. As I recruited, hired, and trained new painters to get them going for the second half of that summer, I treated them completely differently than when I first started running the business. I focused on these things:

- Vision-sharing: I openly shared my vision for the business, and this became our team goal, something we all worked toward together

- Bonuses: I created profit-sharing incentives, in order to ensure my team was aligned with me toward the same goals

- Customer service recognition: I incentivized getting good customer service ratings by turning it into a fun game

- Culture: I organized fun nights out at the bar and paintball gatherings in order to play and socialize together, and I would pick up the tab

- Empathy: I would randomly pop by their job sites on hot days to deliver cold drinks and popsicles—even going so far as to bring a BBQ to a job site where they were working late one evening to grill up some hotdogs and hamburgers for them

Grilling food for my painters.

The results? I was able to retain every one of those painters. Not just for that summer; they stayed with me for the next two and a half years. I ran that business for two more summers, and my painters stayed on because I treated them differently than when I had first started, and they were earning good money, while delivering a quality service and having a great time. I ended up hiring more painters because my business expanded, and most of these new painters were recruited by my existing painters. They encouraged friends to join us since they themselves were enjoying the work and the culture we had created together. And beyond my team being happier, the overall financial improvement was astounding. In my second year, my revenues went up 30 percent, my net profit increased by 120 percent, and I was recognized and awarded "Manager of the Year" for Canada the next two years in a row.

Those early days in my business career were eye-opening and game-changing, and I've always tried to remember the important lessons I learned early on about taking care of your people as a priority and making work more fun.

Note: I did have one painter (Brian Savage) not return the following summer. I had called him to offer him a job again for the coming summer, and he advised me that he had just signed on to play hockey in the NHL with the Montreal Canadiens. His six-figure signing bonus was tough for me, a student entrepreneur, to compete with. Later that summer I landed the contract to paint the clubhouse at the local golf course. You can imagine how painful it was for some of Brian's pals who were still painting for me to see him teeing off on the first tee as they were scraping peeling paint under the hot summer sun. I had to deliver a lot of popsicles to that job site in order to keep the spirits up!

Employee Turnover Can Kill Your Business

John Hall, cofounder of time management app Calendar, took a deep look into turnover. In his *Forbes* article, "The Cost of Turnover Can Kill Your Business and Make Things Less Fun," John points out the following key observations:[4]

- Regardless of the reason, whether due to cutbacks or employee dissatisfaction, frequent turnover carries serious implications for any business.

- Replacing an employee incurs extra costs associated with hiring, interviewing, onboarding,

---

[4] John Hall, "The Cost of Turnover Can Kill Your Business and Make Things Less Fun," *Forbes*, May 9, 2019, https://www.forbes.com/sites /johnhall/2019/05/09/the-cost-of-turnover-can-kill-your-business-and -make-things-less-fun/?sh=43f089f17943.

and more. These costs can include advertising and recruiting fees; travel and time spent interviewing, checking references, and doing background checks; sign-on bonuses; relocation expenses; and training.

- While training, which can take weeks to months, employees are not producing at a high level.

- Personnel directly involved in training new hires are pulled away from other important tasks to focus on bringing new people up to speed.

- You may have to pay your existing employees overtime to pick up the slack during the transition period.

- Morale can suffer, with some workers feeling sad and others wondering if they should leave.

All of these aspects of high turnover can push your business to the breaking point. If your business is financially unprepared to take the hit, it may not survive.

Hall goes on to explain that people will quit because of three main reasons:

1) They don't feel appreciated, or they feel their work and effort go unrecognized

2) They can't handle the workload, and stress becomes too much, enough to drive them away

3) They are experiencing personal issues or strife with coworkers, clients, or managers

Hall's conclusion is that people stick around when their work environment is fun, and they feel satisfied. When we invest time in play and fun in the workplace, our teams feel cared for and appreciated, stress levels get reduced, and we connect on a more fun, personal level with our colleagues, which makes handling the challenging times together a little bit easier. *A fun work environment leads to happy, engaged employees who want to be there, and they end up staying a long time.*

Foster Loyalty
with a Fun Environment

Organizations that provide opportunities for employees to play together, bond as teams, create workplace friendships, and enjoy celebrations (from birthday parties and work anniversaries to potluck lunches, team outings, and scavenger hunts) end up fostering something really valuable: loyalty.

Not only does workplace loyalty inspire people to do their best work and perform to their highest standards, but it also helps reduce turnover.

In my early College Pro Painters days, when I treated my painters like robots, they left. There was no sense of loyalty to me or the business. But when I started to treat them like teammates who I cared about as real people and rewarded their hard work—with financial incentives, games, social events, or even something as simple as cold popsicles on a hot day—loyalty and productivity skyrocketed.

A Strong Culture Can Win Employees Back

As this *Harvard Business Review* article points out and as is fairly common knowledge in the business world,[5] it is often more valuable to attempt to win back a disgruntled customer than it is to find new customers. Some reasons for this include the following:

---

[5] Angus Greig, "Winning Back Lost Customers," *Harvard Business Review,* March 2016, https://hbr.org/2016/03/winning-back-lost-customers.

- These customers have already demonstrated a desire for the service and are thus better prospects than a cold call

- They are familiar with the company, eliminating the need to create brand awareness and educate them about the offering and, thus, reducing the cost of marketing to them

- Technology and sophisticated customer databases allow companies to draw on information about how former customers used their service the first time around to craft more successful win-back offers and to identify and go after the most profitable defectors

Well, the same can be true about strong employees who may have left your organization. And while a strong culture can go a long way to helping retain employees *before* they leave, sometimes we do lose them for reasons outside our control. But believe it or not, occasionally we can also—again, by virtue of a strong culture, which helps create a special loyalty with employees—win them back *after* they leave.

Ever since the COVID-19 pandemic triggered the Great Resignation, or The Big Quit as some are calling it, with high numbers of employees voluntarily leaving their jobs due to shifting goals and the search for something different or better, there's no getting around the fact that despite your best efforts, you may wind up losing some great people.

This happened to us at JAM. We lost some key team members during the pandemic. But that's not the end of the story. Here's what happened.

Sandeep

One of our top people and an all-around great guy, Sandeep, had been working for JAM for over six and a half years. He started out as an operations associate. Then, after about a year, he moved into bookkeeping to cover someone going on maternity leave, and from there he grew into one of the leaders of our finance team. Sandeep has a great wit, is hard-working, humble, an incredible athlete (always a bonus to have him on our corporate sports teams), and easily one of the most ethical and trustworthy people I know. He contributed so much to our fun company culture; everyone loved having him on the team.

And Sandeep loved being a part of our organization. In addition to being excited and driven in general by our company's purpose of connecting people through play, he was also passionate about his work specifically, as he knew what he was doing would help make a positive impact in the lives of others.

Then, in the middle of the pandemic, Sandeep reached the difficult decision to leave our company for a job elsewhere that paid more and that he felt would give him new experiences. We were heartbroken. It was a heavy conversation between Sandeep and the rest of our team because none of us wanted to see him go. He was very gracious, taking the time to help us through the transition, and making himself available for questions long after he had off-boarded since he knew what a huge part of the organization he had become. I made sure to tell him when he left, "While we are sad to see you leave, we wish you only the best, and please know, there will always be a spot for you on our team if you ever decide you want to come back."

Fast forward nine months, and I'm thrilled to report that Sandeep has returned to JAM. A few weeks after rejoining our team, he wrote me a text that said, "I am so happy to be back. It's unbelievable. I should never have left."

So what happened between him leaving and then coming back from what we now affectionately refer to as his "sabbatical"?

After leaving JAM for a higher-paying job with great responsibilities, very quickly, he discovered in his new workplace a complete lack of culture. Everyone went to work, did their job, and went home. There were no real interactions or friendships between coworkers, no opportunities for play, no fun. Nobody did anything socially together at all. Apparently, people didn't even talk nicely to each other. Nobody expressed any degree of curiosity about their coworkers. Further, Sandeep found himself questioning the integrity of the operations. Most of all, he realized he was not driven by the new organization's purpose—so while he was indeed earning more money, he wasn't happy. It was a very depressing environment.

After working in his new role for four months, Sandeep decided enough was enough. He didn't want to feel like he was selling his soul just for a big paycheck. He realized that no amount of money was worth working at a place that didn't seem to care about its people or culture. He handed in his letter of resignation with no other job to go to.

Several months later, the right spot opened up at our organization, and we were able to bring Sandeep back. When our team heard he was returning, everyone was thrilled. *People are happier when they are working with colleagues they consider teammates and friends.*

So the great news is that Sandeep is back on our team again. And when I recently saw a promotional piece that our marketing team had created to promote our beach volleyball leagues, which had Sandeep's smiling face on it, I said to him, "Dude, not only are you back on our team, but now you're the face of our organization—this makes me so happy!"

Sandeep

Taylor

The neat thing is, Sandeep's story is not a unique one for our organization. Taylor Lewis joined our team as the manager for our newly created not-for-profit foundation Keep

Playing Kids (1 percent of all JAM revenue goes toward helping underserved youth in our communities play sports for free) only a few months before the pandemic completely shut down our operations.

Once the pandemic hit, and we were mandated to stop operating both our adult sports leagues and our newly launched kids foundation, Taylor showed a willingness to lean into the changes going on and work in a variety of areas with us in order to help our organization survive. As JAM pivoted into running corporate virtual team-bonding events all over the globe, Taylor remained hard-working, open-minded, and optimistic—and she became the first account coordinator for this new vertical we had created. While corporate virtual events for team-bonding were quite different from connecting underserved youth through the playing of sports, Taylor was still excited that we had found a way to help people connect through play.

After a year or so of working in this new area of our business, Taylor was offered an opportunity at another organization in a totally different industry. This company was offering more compensation than we could compete with, as well as a different career opportunity that Taylor was interested in pursuing. So she made the difficult decision to leave our team.

Fast forward seven months: Taylor saw a job posting for her old position at JAM and applied to come back. Our HR team was ecstatic to see her application for the role and after some deep discussions made the decision to welcome her back to our team.

Taylor recently shared with me that when she was a couple months into her new job, although she was earning more money, she could feel her mental health taking a turn for the worse. She didn't have a passion for the organization's purpose, and she had recognized how important it was for her own mental health that she work at a place where the purpose was inspiring to her. She also discovered how much better it is to work with a team who knows how to prioritize play and fun even when there is a lot of hard work to be done, because doing so is what improves human connections, friendships, and bonds among colleagues. JAM's focus on a playful culture won Taylor back.

Culture Made the Difference

I love Sandeep and Taylor's stories, not only because we got a couple of great teammates back on our team, but also because it demonstrates just how important culture is. *Often, culture can be more important than money.*

In a fun work culture where there are genuine friendships, people stay. And even if they do leave for a new opportunity, if the new culture they encounter isn't strong they may wish they hadn't left and want to come back. Sandeep and Taylor both loved being on our team. They each left for all the right personal reasons. But in the end, our culture brought them back. We care about our people. We have friends within our workplace. We have fun together. And this was enough for Sandeep to walk away from a high-paying but soul-killing job and for Taylor to leave a job she knew was negatively impacting her mental health in order to come back to our team.

Having said that, if you want to incentivize strong people to join your team, you need to be prepared to reward them financially as well. If your business can afford to do so, ideally you will do both—pay competitive, generous salaries while also striving to foster a strong, fun work culture.

When it comes to influencing someone's decision to join or stay with your team, never underestimate the importance of a purpose-driven organization with a strong, fun workplace culture—especially a culture that values play and fosters strong personal friendships and relationships among its team.

You May Not Want to Hire People Straight Out of University

I'm going to share something that may sound a little controversial to some leaders out there: Our organization generally tries to avoid hiring people straight out of college. We prefer hiring folks who've had experience working in one or two other places first. That way, when they join our team, they realize, *Wow! This is nothing like that other place where I used to work. The culture here is amazing!*

I've learned that Barry Glassman—founder of Glassman Wealth Services, a highly successful investment, financial, and wealth planning solutions firm—has the same philosophy. Glassman's company makes it a point to hire people from their competitors, so that when they join, they can say, "Holy shit, this organization is so much more fun! This is what it's like to work at a place where the people care about their people."

At Glassman Wealth, Barry says "booking 'fun' in the calendar once a quarter does not feel authentic." Rather, he believes play and fun should be a constant. Over the years, Glassman Wealth has had a softball team, bowling team, wine dinners, BBQs at the boss's house—and they always find fun ways to celebrate their successes. Barry says, "We are a curious group, which explains why we have played in so many JAM virtual events—and kicked butt at '80s trivia even though the average age of our employees is only thirty-five—as well as why we have a 'puzzle table' in our office. It's because we like to playfully explore and challenge ourselves."

Barry also believes that a playful culture directly benefits clients. Which means *everyone* benefits: employees, customers, the organization, and its bottom line. (More on this in Chapter 6.)

Glassman Wealth has been recognized by the *Washington Business Journal* as the number one best place to work in Washington, DC an impressive three times. And in eleven years, the company has had zero employees leave to work for a competitor. If that isn't loyalty, I don't know what is.

How PLAY Factors into Loyalty and Retention

The presence of play in the workplace breeds connections and friendships and strengthens bonds. When we play together, we get to know one another on a more personal level, and this is how friendships and bonds develop and improve. When you have people who feel strongly bonded to their teammates, they're more loyal to your organization.

Our employees have always had the option to join teams and play in our adult recreational sports leagues for free. This was an easy way for our organization to provide a fun, healthy opportunity for employees to socially connect and develop friendships with each other. When they played soccer or beach volleyball or trivia together, they were able to get to know one another at a different level personally than when they were in a meeting talking about the business or reviewing spreadsheets.

When employees get to know each other on a more personal and fun level, and share some laughs together, they also become more empathetic and supportive and more willing to try to help one another. They can communicate more easily and show more vulnerability as they work together to solve problems that arise in your business.

Many of my own teammates will tell you how during busy periods at JAM, they all tend to check in with each other—either verbally if working together in person, or by chat message if working remotely—before wrapping up for the day. They do this as a way of seeing if anyone needs help finishing up time-sensitive work. This type of team-player behavior wouldn't exist to nearly the same degree were it not for the strong connections and friendships we have fostered.

Whether an organization is working in-person, hybrid, or fully remotely, when these personal connections have been tended to, employees are more apt to feel good about the organization they're working for.

Like Kids in School

When you were a child, having good friends to spend time with made you look forward to getting on that school bus in the morning. You were excited to see them and have fun together. But if you *didn't* have good friends, you probably weren't as happy about going to school. Growing up, we've all had those times when we've felt a little lost or sad at school because our friends weren't treating us well, or best friends moved away, or we found ourselves dodging bullies.

Strong friendships helped to make school enjoyable; a climate of hostility or isolation made us want to stay home.

Guess what? Nothing's changed. It's the same equation for adults in the workplace.

Simply put, having connections and friendships makes us feel good. Strong bonds at work make us happy to be there, which in turn makes us more loyal to our colleagues and the company.

> When you're happy at work, it makes you want to stay and keep doing better.

Don't Expect Employees to Stay Forever, but Aim for Several Years

This isn't the 1950s. People *do* move around between companies. It's unrealistic to expect employees to stay at your organization for twenty or thirty years. That's rare these days.

But it's not unreasonable to hope they stay with you ten, twelve, maybe fifteen years. A strong workplace culture focused on people playing and having fun together can help make this a reality.

At JAM, we seek to celebrate loyalty among our team. When our teammates hit their one-year mark with us, we celebrate with an official "draft ceremony," signifying that they are officially drafted as a "veteran" onto our team. Vets receive a hockey jersey with the company logo on front and their name across the back. The number on the jersey symbolizes the year they started with us. This is a small token, but it creates a lot of pride for the vets on our team to have their jersey hanging on their office chair or on the wall at their home office. We also celebrate teammates who have been with us for three, five, ten, fifteen years, and more with special anniversary gifts that are unique to them. This month alone we celebrated a five-, ten-, and fifteen-year anniversary for three different teammates. Every organization can have their own unique way of celebrating—it doesn't need to be costly or complicated—but the point is to leverage the power of a fun celebration to acknowledge a teammate's loyalty.

As we've learned in this chapter, the last thing you want is for someone to start working at your business only to leave six or nine months down the road. This type of turnover is a waste of everyone's time and energy, and it's expensive. You've spent too much investing in building this person up to be of service to your organization to have them go elsewhere. Having a fun, playful culture that helps keep amazing people on your team, as well as potentially win some back, absolutely pays dividends when it comes to loyalty and retention.

Chapter 1 Key Takeaway Points

→ High turnover is expensive, demoralizing, and time-consuming and should be avoided whenever possible

→ Fun and play help friendships and bonds develop between coworkers

→ When people have friends at work, they're more invested in their jobs and more motivated to do their best for each other

→ While play is not the only factor that can solve the problem of high employee turnover (money still matters), play is an important and easily implemented factor that improves culture and often gets overlooked

→ Having meaningful friendships at work makes people want to stay (and possibly return if they do leave), reducing turnover and simultaneously fostering loyalty

The good news is that employees who play together and feel strong connections to others at work are happier, making them more likely to stick around. Less turnover creates more stability and benefits both the health of the entire team and the bottom line of the organization.

In addition to helping with loyalty and retention, making time for play at work can also increase engagement and morale among your staff, as we'll see in the next chapter.

PLAY Increases Engagement

*"This is the real secret of life—
to be completely engaged with what you are
doing in the here and now. And instead of
calling it work, realize it is play."*

—ALAN WATTS

How engaged are employees with their work?

It might shock you to learn that, according to a recent Gallup poll, only 36 percent of employees feel engaged in the workplace.[6] That's a pretty sad statistic. *Employee engagement is the emotional commitment an employee has to the organization and its goals.* An engaged employee doesn't just work for a paycheck, or for the next promotion, but rather they work on behalf of the organization's goals because they are motivated by the purpose and the culture.

If only 36 percent of people are engaged by their work and excited about their workplace culture, then a staggering 64 percent are disengaged, unmotivated, and uncommitted.

Look at your workplace. How many employees do you have?

- If six people are working for you, statistics show that only two are fully engaged in what they're doing.

- If you have twenty-five employees, nine are engaged; a whopping sixteen employees are disengaged.

- If you have a thousand employees, only 360

---

6   Jim Harter, "US Employee Engagement Reverts Back to Pre-COVID-19 Levels," *Gallup,* October 16, 2020, https://www.gallup.com/workplace /321965/employee-engagement-reverts-back-pre-covid-levels.aspx.

are engaged. The remaining 640 are not meeting their potential because they're unmotivated and unenthusiastic about work.

If we look at that twenty-five-person team as an example and assume an average $50,000 salary, this means $800,000 of a total $1.25 million payroll is being spent on staff who are not engaged or motivated. Having such a high percentage of employees at your organization who don't care about their jobs or your company is a massive waste of resources and potential. Your customers and your engaged employees deserve better, and your business won't be able to thrive at a higher level with such a lack of engagement.

According to the Latest Gallup Report

A closer look at the numbers paints an even starker picture.

The 64 percent of the workforce that's disengaged can be split up further into two groups: "not engaged" and "actively disengaged."

"Not engaged" means that they're psychologically unattached to their jobs and on the lookout for something better. This group makes up 51 percent of the workforce—over half!

"Actively disengaged" means they're miserable at work and, like a virus, most likely spreading this unhappiness to coworkers and customers. This group makes up 13 percent of the workforce.

WORKFORCE ENGAGEMENT

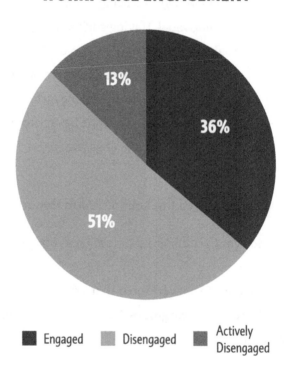

So if you have a hundred employees, thirty-six are engaged, fifty-one are disengaged and ready to quit at a moment's notice, and thirteen are super unhappy and quite possibly actively poisoning your workplace culture.

I certainly don't want these stats to be true in my organization, and I'm sure you don't want them for yours either. To shift the balance and get more of your people actively engaged at work, you have to take the lead and show them that they matter and that you care.

Results from The Employee Experience Imperative Report[7] have shown that when employers work to create meaningful experiences for their staff, they will benefit from a more engaged and productive workforce. Researchers also found that employees generally wanted to provide feedback to their managers and employers, but they often felt like their suggestions were falling on deaf ears.

At JAM, we know that play can be a simple and cost-effective way to create fun, meaningful experiences among our team and that doing so will help to strengthen personal connections and relationships. Colleagues who feel

---

[7] "Research Report: The Employee Experience Imperative," Service Now, accessed May 12, 2022, https://www.servicenow.com/lpwhp/employee -experience-imperative.html?cid=pr:employee_experience_research.

a stronger personal connection with their managers will have an easier time communicating candidly and honestly and will be more apt to feel heard by their leaders. Making a little time for play in the workplace will show your teammates that you care about them as people, that they matter, beyond just the work they deliver.

Profitability Goes Up with Engaged Workers

To be honest, I was very surprised to learn that only 36 percent of workers feel engaged with one another and the work they're doing. It's heartbreaking, especially considering the average person will spend one third of their life at work.[8]

Another Gallup report statistic that doesn't surprise me and makes me feel a little more optimistic[9] informs us that a highly engaged workforce increases profitability. This Gallup study confirmed that employee engagement continues to

---

[8] "One Third of Your Life is Spent at Work," Gettysburg College, accessed May 12, 2022, https://www.gettysburg.edu/news/stories?id=79db7b34 -630c-4f49-ad32-4ab9ea48e72b.

[9] Susan Sorenson, "How Employee Engagement Drives Growth," *Gallup*, June 20, 2013, https://www.gallup.com/workplace/236927/employee -engagement-drives-growth.aspx.

be an important predictor of company performance even in a tough economy. Work units ranked in the top quartile of employee engagement outperform bottom-quartile units in profitability by 22 percent. That's a significant upturn and a great opportunity!

When your team members are engaged with one another, their work, and the customers they serve, of course your company is going to be better off. Engaged teams are that much more caring, and they deliver better service, keep costs down, and are more willing to help out their teammates.

Productivity Goes Up Too

The Gallup report also notes that companies with highly engaged workforces have 21 percent higher productivity than companies with disengaged workforces. Engaged employees have bought into what the organization is about and are actively trying to make a difference. This is why they are usually the most productive workers.

If these statistics aren't enough, here are more reasons to do everything in your power to increase engagement among your employees:

- Engaged employees are motivated to complete their tasks on time and successfully

- They go the extra mile to reach their goals and objectives

- They are happier overall, have fewer absences, and are generally more loyal to the organization

- They report better health outcomes

- They're better at meeting customers' needs, leading to more sales and higher revenues

When it comes down to it, this is really a no-brainer: if you want healthier, happier employees who take fewer sick days, are more productive, and interact better with clients, then you need to foster a workplace culture that makes people want to be there and give their best effort every day.

A Different Kind of Engagement than What You're Used To

Traditionally, when experts talk about building great cultures, they focus on the importance of engaging one's teams around purpose, vision, and values. While I wholeheartedly agree that these are critical pillars, I would also suggest there is more we can and ought to be doing in order to help our teammates feel engaged. In addition to feeling bought into an organization's purpose, vision, and values, employees want to feel engaged and friendly with the people they work with day in and day out.

> In addition to engaging with ideas, employees want to engage directly with the people they work with day after day.

It's a basic human impulse to want to connect with the people around us. When we're at work, we want to engage not just over job-related matters as company employees, but on a much more personal level as well. We want to get to know our coworkers as human beings and bond with them.

One of the easiest ways to encourage these bonds—and in turn, increase engagement—is through play.

Friendship Is a Key to Greater Engagement

Making time for play is incredibly powerful because that's when friendships form. And when friendships develop, connections build. When employees are strongly bonded, they're much more inclined to help one another out. They *want* to support their teammates, and so they show up in a way that's much more present and engaged.

Sometimes you'll find team members having friendly competitions over who can make the most sales. Or if a profit-sharing plan is in place, employees will feel even more compelled to make the business a better place for *everyone* because they know all will benefit. There's no end to the advantages that come with workplace friendships.

And fostering a workplace culture where these types of bonds are free to develop is a lot simpler than many business leaders realize! I'll provide some ideas and examples at the end of the book for affordable and easy-to-implement ways to foster a fun, playful workplace culture.

Research Backs the Need for PLAY at Work

In their article "Playing Up the Benefits of Play at Work,"[10] the Association for Psychological Science (APS) reports on

---

[10] "Playing Up the Benefits of Play at Work," Association for Psychological Science, October 13, 2017, https://www.psychologicalscience.org/news /minds-business/playing-up-the-benefits-of-play-at-work.html.

research conducted on the powerful benefits for both the individual and the organization when we make time for play at work. APS challenges conventional wisdom or popular notions that suggest work is work, play is play, and never the two shall mix. On the contrary, APS points out how scientific research backs up the need to play at work for a whole range of benefits.

According to the article, researchers have found evidence that play at work is tied to all of the following:

- Less boredom and fatigue

- Less stress

- More job satisfaction

- A sense of competence

- Higher levels of individual and organizational creativity

- More engagement in tasks that are presented playfully

- Greater trust and stronger bonds

- Increased social interactions and friendly work atmosphere

- A sense of solidarity and a decreased sense of hierarchy

- Higher commitment to one's job

Leaders, take note: a playful work culture which strengthens employee engagement is in your organization's best interest. With happier, more engaged people raising the company's level of productivity, you can achieve the growth you want faster while getting the reputation for being an awesome company that everyone wants to work for.

Integrating Playful Events, Complete with Budgets

My brilliant friend Kara Goldin is the founder and CEO of Hint, a natural fruit-flavored water brand with the purpose of helping people lead healthier lives. Kara recently introduced me to her senior director of HR, Tracy Kasin.

Tracy started working at Hint in 2017 when there were roughly sixty people on the team. The company has since grown to about two hundred people. Tracy describes Hint's culture as "passionate." Employees are hardworking and entrepreneurial, and company leaders recognize the importance and benefits of making time for fun and play.

Our JAM team had the pleasure of hosting the entire Hint organization in Name That Tune bingo and trivia games for their virtual holiday event, where the laughs were plenty. But Hint doesn't make time for fun only during the holidays. They integrate playful, fun events at a variety of levels at different times year-round. These range from full, company-wide events to specific department events.

And here's the really important part: since Kara is passionate about people and culture, team leaders at Hint have their own *budgets* to ensure they make time for playful connection with their teams. They are provided with financial resources to integrate playful events into the workplace, making play a key part of their corporate culture.

Finally, it should be noted that just because an organization has a budget for investment in play does not mean it needs to be huge amounts of money. Having a budget for play and culture shows intention toward strengthening engagement. There are many easy and budget-friendly ways to do this, and I will share a number of different ideas at the end of the book. Empowering leaders culturally and financially shows that the company cares about their people and ensures they are engaged with each other and the organization.

Newfound Enthusiasm and a Higher Level of Trust

Kara and her team at Hint also put into place an annual internship opportunity called the "Hintern" program—the name alone shows a playful attitude. The Hintern program incorporated a number of playful events, in a variety of locations around the country. These included fishing in Florida, golfing in the Northeast, heading to a ballgame in Chicago, and karaoke in Texas. Feedback from the various events was overwhelmingly positive, and photos clearly showed so much fun being had as teams connected playfully with their new interns and their full-time employees.

Hint team fishing.

Hint team at the ball game.

Tracy explained that each team set up its own event, and none were overly expensive, time-consuming, or complex. Every participating team benefited greatly, with team members gaining newfound enthusiasm and a higher, more trusting level of engagement with one another.

Tracy also stresses that it's great to *have the C-suite folks join in the fun.* Morale climbs when CEO Kara or COO Theo attend these fun events. The entire Hint team gets to know these leaders more personally, finding out, for example, that Kara loves her dogs, cares about her garden, and loves to share fun stories about her four kids. Getting to know everyone from the CEO to the interns at a more human level helps build trust, engagement, and morale.

Hint hosts company-wide playful events typically on a monthly basis. Because team leaders have their own budgets, many teams also do their own fun events every six weeks or so. Play is not an afterthought. It's embedded in the passionate culture at Hint.

Morale and Engagement Go Hand in Hand

The concept of morale is closely related to engagement. In organizations where morale is high, employees look forward to going to work every day. They're more engaged with their teammates and the tasks that need to get done.

When you give employees the chance to engage with one another through play, more friendships develop at work, and you tend to see a huge boost in morale across the board.

An employee who is engaged tends to do the following:

- Care about the organization's purpose and vision

- Share or resonate with the company's values

- Feel happier and closer with their teammates

- Enjoy their job more and want to be at work and do their best for each other

- Perform at a higher level

Can you see how getting more of your employees feeling engaged can boost morale company-wide? The two really do go hand in hand.

One Bad Apple Can Ruin the Bunch

One team member who is miserable and actively disengaged can very quickly bring morale down, similarly to how one rotting apple in a barrel can spread decay to all the rest. You need to get poison out of your organization, and you need it out fast, because it can really ruin culture for everyone.

Over our last twenty-five years operating JAM, we've learned this the hard way...more than once. In the past, we've been slow to let a "bad apple" go and have paid the price a few times. We've seen firsthand how one unhappy employee may trigger one or two other good teammates to leave and may hurt relationships with important partners along the way.

At one point we had a team leader—I'll call him John—who started off strong and was a fantastic addition to our team. John brought great knowledge and experience to our organization and added great value for a few years. While far from perfect (after all, no human is), overall John was a strong leader and mentor to his team. And to his higher-ups, John always appeared willing to go above and beyond and work very hard, rolling up his sleeves and digging in to help the organization however he could, which was always greatly appreciated.

In time, something changed, and to this day I'm not really sure what. John started postponing or canceling meetings with his direct reports at the last minute. We also noticed that when John made mistakes, he would rarely apologize or own them as his own errors and instead would often blame others. More and more, drama seemed to be coming from John's department.

When two of John's direct reports bypassed John and came to the leadership team directly in order to share their concerns, we made the mistake of only partially listening. We reorganized their department so that they would report to others instead of John, which was less than ideal, but we didn't dig deeper into why the drama was happening. That's because we wanted John to keep up the valued work we felt *he* was doing for our organization. So we continued to work and meet with John separately, thinking perhaps he was still engaged and keen but just didn't want to manage people the same way he had initially.

John's "blame game" seemed to worsen after this, and the drama only increased. Eventually, one of John's direct reports, Ellen, resigned. We were devastated by this news because Ellen was such a hard worker and a strong cultural fit with our team. We could also tell that two of John's other reports were visibly unhappy, yet we were still somewhat blind as to *why* they were less than fully engaged.

In retrospect, we allowed John's negativity to fester for much too long. Even after Ellen had resigned and had been gone from JAM for six months, John would still continue to play the "blame game," frequently blaming Ellen for any issue that arose. Clearly, he had become toxic.

We finally opened our eyes to our need to part ways with John, likely twelve to eighteen months later than we should have. Then, after we parted ways, I was surprised to hear comments from some of our other teammates, like "I think you were the only person that John was ever nice to." We also received negative comments from outside suppliers: "John was good at what he did, but he was always so rude to our staff, we never enjoyed working with him."

While we couldn't change the damage that had already been done in terms of tarnished relationships with suppliers, or the loss of a great teammate like Ellen, we *could* work to build back trust with John's remaining direct reports and rebuild respectful relationships with our suppliers. And that's exactly what we did. Now, we try to always remember and learn from situations like this, taking much swifter action when such issues arise. Granted, this can sometimes be easier said than done, especially when, like with John, an employee delivers great value in some ways while potentially poisoning your culture in others. The reality is this: any amount of poison is too much if you want to have a healthy organizational culture.

Remember, if the average is true, and 13 percent of your employees are "actively disengaged," this is the type of damage that can be occurring under your own nose. One bad apple can truly ruin the whole bunch if you allow its poison to fester inside your organization.

It is critical that team leaders have regular touch points

with their employees and teams in order to be aware of any potential discontent brewing. If someone is miserable, don't fool yourself into thinking that it's just a problem with that one person. If you do nothing, the bad vibes will spread. Don't allow that to happen. Take action quickly and continue to work to improve your culture through fun and play, which will help strengthen and improve communications and bonds for all.

People Breathe Life into Purpose, Vision, and Values

As a company leader, you've got your organization's purpose, vision, and values firmly established and written down in documents such as a Vision Statement. Not only have you helped put these into place, but you study them, keep them in focus, and work hard to get everyone on board.

But here's what you have to remember: these are just concepts until people make them happen. People are the ones who breathe life into your ideas. Without prioritizing your people, nothing happens.

So in order for your purpose, vision, and values to come to life, you have to invest in your people. You have to motivate them and create opportunities for playful fun that creates the friendships that will help employees stay more engaged.

Why is this so important? In the end, the people engaging with your ideas and with one another are the same individuals who will help turn your vision into reality.

Twice a Year We Ask Our Employees This

At JAM, we make a point of checking in with our teammates twice a year, to ask one very important question:

"What's your favorite thing about working with us?"

The number one answer is always the same: our team.

It's the friendships. Over the years, this has been a constant theme. We have a great team of people who are fun and engaged. And because of our focus on incorporating play to build connections within our own team, we've been able to maintain a strong culture.

That said, a word of caution is needed here. You can't expect people to be engaged *all the time*, or to give their absolute best every second they're working for you. Inevitably, there will be moments of disinterest, frustration, and dissatisfaction. That's normal. We all have our occasional down day or week.

But looking at the big picture, you can see who is generally engaged and who isn't. On more than one occasion, I've had to make the difficult decision to let go of someone who isn't engaged. It's never fun, but it's necessary to nip the problem in the bud before the employee poisons the culture. Thankfully, the vast majority of the people at our organization love working where they are, and they repeatedly rank the following as top reasons to work with us:

- People

- Culture

- Purpose

- Vision

- Growth opportunity

The core purpose of our organization is to help people connect through play. Those who work on our team actively support and genuinely benefit from this focus. We've always had a playful culture, and this works for us. It can work for you too.

Keeping It Simple

At JAM, we connect people through play, and we help companies profit through play. Our vision for JAM is to get one million people playing annually. It's a big goal to chase, but we are committed to making it happen. Our leadership team checks in with one another regularly to ensure we are moving along the right track. We ask ourselves and encourage our teammates to always ask themselves these questions:

- Is what I'm doing right now going to help get one million people playing?

- If not, why am I doing it?

Constantly checking in with our shared vision—and holding up what we're doing against it—keeps us all rowing the boat in the same direction. We keep our goal simple and clear, which helps everyone to stay on track.

Many people think it is easy to keep play a priority in our workplace because play is the service we sell. The truth is, play is serious business to us, and we work incredibly hard as a team, but we also know how to make time for fun. And I know that regardless of whether your company is selling life insurance, manufacturing steel cables, or providing digital marketing expertise, making a little time for play in your workplace can be done and will pay dividends. It really doesn't matter what your organization is involved in. The goal is still the same: ensuring your teammates feel engaged.

You want to engage your employees to get them behind your vision, and you can increase engagement by creating ways for your people to connect with one another in meaningful ways. *Whatever your company vision is, never lose sight of the importance of fostering personal connections to increase company engagement.*

Revisit Your Company Values

At JAM, we have six core values:

1) Chase the vision

2) Deliver what you promise

3) Take pride in what you do

4) Treat everyone like your best friend

5) Get shit done

6) Find a better way

These are serious values that keep our company going, but they're presented in a playful way. We constantly keep these values at the top of our minds, and every decision we make gets vetted against these values. If any of my team members ever struggles with a decision, all they have to do is ask: Am I delivering what I promise? Am I treating everyone like my best friend? Am I finding a better way?

In other words, whatever important decision we need to make, we hold it up against our core values. Doing this makes our jobs a lot easier.

In addition to having our core values written on the walls around our office and on a mouse pad that every teammate gets, we celebrate them with a monthly core value award. At the end of every month, we send out our core value award survey to the entire team. We encourage everybody to nominate someone as a way of highlighting how people are living the values in their jobs. The survey is short, simply asking for the name of who is being nominated, along with the value they are excelling at and a short blurb as to why they are being nominated. Once all the nominations are gathered by our HR team, we get them into a slide presentation, which I then share and read out at huddle once a month.

This presentation—where we read all the nominations and celebrate our winner—usually takes ten or fifteen minutes, and it is worth every moment. It's an opportunity to shine a light on all the great work being done by members of our team. In particular, it allows one teammate to give a gift of gratitude and recognition and another to receive a gift of the spotlight for work well done.

JAM Core Value Award

Normally, the teammate with the most nominations in the month receives the core value award trophy. I'm such a literal and visual person, I got a trophy made to look like an apple core. It stands about eighteen inches tall and has our six core values listed around the base. And now that many of us are working remotely more often, we also give the winner a special Core Value Award Zoom backdrop which only they get to use at our daily huddle (or any other meetings they may have all month).

When your employees are engaged in the company's purpose, vision, and values, as well as with one another, you end up with a powerful company culture that's strengthened by high levels of morale. And when you have that, your organization can become an unstoppable force for good. Everybody wins.

Our Seven-Minute Huddle

If part or all of your workforce is working remotely, you may be struggling with coming up with ways to increase engagement and connection. One solution we implemented at JAM is our virtual, seven-minute daily huddle. A daily huddle is an idea inspired by my friend Brian Scudamore who is the CEO and founder of 1-800-GOT-JUNK? and O2E brands. At

O2E brands they take culture seriously, and they don't just talk the talk. I take every opportunity I can to learn from Brian and his team.

We set our daily huddle at 1:00 p.m. EST, which has allowed everyone on our team to jump on the call, no matter where they are living and working or whether they are working shifted afternoon/evening hours. We have had teammates working from Toronto, Paris, Vancouver, Edmonton, Kitchener–Waterloo, Ottawa, Michigan, Texas, and Costa Rica. Having this daily connection provides everyone the opportunity to connect—across departments, levels, and geographies. Each person on our team, from co-op student or intern to president or CEO, takes a turn leading the huddle. We encourage everyone to have their cameras on, so we can all see one another's faces and smiles.

At huddle, we share the following:

- Good News (both personal and business)

- Important Metrics

- Departmental Updates (we hear from a different department each day of the week)

- Last Call (an opportunity for anyone to share anything important)

- Clarity Questions (in case anyone has a question)

- Cascading Messages (this is where we highlight critical items we want to ensure are sent by email for those who may have missed huddle)

- Leader's Choice (always a surprise, fun finish)

The daily leader ends huddle in their own way, maybe sharing a little trivia about outer space or whales, or perhaps encouraging everyone to do thirty sit-ups or go for a fifteen-minute outdoor walk that day, or maybe telling a joke or asking everyone to post a photo from their first sports team in our banter channel. Every day is a new surprise. And often the stories shared at huddle or in the banter channel afterward have kept our team laughing long after the huddle is over.

As an example, one time the Leader's Choice was to share a funny memory in the group chat about being a freshman in college or university. Sandeep (whom I talked about in Chapter 1) shared this story with everyone:

We had a Frosh Week challenge at U of T, where the freshmen had to attempt to get through a stone archway to retrieve an object on a pillar on the other side. The archway and pillar were heavily guarded by all the frosh leaders, who resorted to all means necessary to keep us out. I showed up in a Speedo and swimming cap, absolutely doused in baby oil. I launched myself into the fray and eeled my way through the crowd. I ended up with a black eye because I landed on my face and ended up covered in some unknown person's vomit that actually really stuck to the baby oil, but I did get the prize in record time. Suffice to say, the tradition was discontinued the following year.

Recently, another Leader's Choice was for each of us to share in our group chat about a time anyone may have won a silly award in grade school or high school and describe the award. After huddle, the chat went wild, lighting up with hilarious anecdotes like these:

- Andrew: "I was a drummer in a band in high school that won our Battle of the Bands at the local fall fair—we were the only band who entered."

- Tanisha: "Grade 4: Best Handwriting."

- Drew: "Grade 11, I was awarded Senior Male Athlete of the Year. This was the peak of my sporting career until I joined our company floor hockey team 'Team Balls.'"

- Eric: "Grade 7 French award—pretty easy win after transferring out of a French-immersion public school. My poor classmates stood no chance."

- And perhaps my favorite share from our lead developer, Brian: "In Grade 3, I was using the library computer and thought it would be funny to install a system extension that made the computer randomly emit burping noises. A few days go by, and I am called to the principal's office. My mom is already there—never a good sign. They explain to me that what I have done is not funny, but that nobody on staff knows how to make the library computer stop burping. So they take me to the library, and I make it stop burping, which I found to be hilarious, much to the chagrin of everyone else. Later my Grade 3 teacher (who was kind of a computer nerd) gave me a little printout celebrating the achievement. Even he didn't know how I'd done it."

So as you can imagine, this simple seven-minute daily huddle accomplishes a lot in a short time. We pass important updates on to our team, while also enjoying some laughs and playful human connection with each other. It costs us nothing except seven minutes each day, yet it allows us to get to know each other better as friends. Taking this time to chat and laugh together makes a huge, positive difference to everyone in our organization. To get a sample huddle agenda and/or to see a video of our JAM huddle in action go to kristiherold.com/resources.

Chapter 2 Key Takeaway Points

→ Employees who are engaged at work tend to be happier, more motivated, more connected, more productive, and more likely to stick around.

→ Happier employees who feel a connection with their peers boost morale across the board, which can also increase the company's profitability and productivity

→ Actively disengaged employees bring others down and degrade the workplace culture

→ Research shows that play at work leads to greater job satisfaction, a friendlier work environment, and a higher level of dedication to one's job

→ Creating fun connections at work that boost engagement can be simple and not overly complicated or costly

Happier, engaged employees are also more likely to stay physically and mentally healthy. This benefits them, and it helps your organization stay strong even in the face of unexpected global developments.

PLAY Improves Health

"There is no real difference between
work and play—it's all living."

—RICHARD BRANSON

According to studies conducted by the Mayo Clinic,[11] combining your exercise regimen with play, by enjoying highly social sports like tennis or soccer, will add five to ten years to your life.

---

[11] Peter Schnohr, et al., "Various Leisure-Time Physical Activities Associated with Widely Divergent Life Expectancies: The Copenhagen City Heart Study," Mayo Clinic Proceedings, December 1, 2018, https://www.mayo clinicproceedings.org/article/S0025-6196(18)30538-X/references.

We all know that exercise on its own offers great benefits for your cardiovascular health, blood sugar levels, bone strength, endurance, weight, mood, and so much more. But the Mayo Clinic saw that physical activity isn't the only factor to consider. When you add a social component, as well as a measure of fun, you get better results than you would from exercise alone.

Working out in your home gym or taking power walks on your own at lunch is great—pretty much any type of exercise will benefit your health. But varying up your exercise to include play, which in turn means engaging and interacting with others, can literally add years to your life. The Mayo Clinic research also found that playing team sports—i.e., ones that involve social connectivity—produce greater longevity than individual sports. Interestingly, the leisure-time sports that inherently involve more social interaction—like tennis, badminton, and soccer—were associated with the greatest longevity.

ADDED YEARS OF LIFE VS SEDENTARY LIFESTYLE

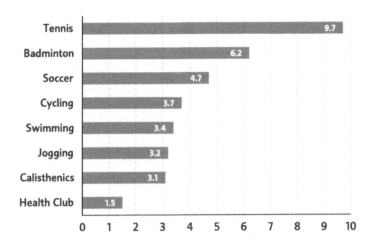

Given this information, team sports and group activities like the following are fantastic for your overall health and well-being:

- Tennis, racquetball, badminton, squash, and pickleball

- Soccer

- Volleyball

- Basketball

- Flag football

- Ultimate frisbee

- Ball hockey or ice hockey

- Softball

- Kickball

- Dodgeball

- Dance classes

- Musical theater

- Yoga, spin, and fitness classes

- And many other group sports and activities

But what does this have to do with your employees?

Everything.

The fact is that more fun in the workplace leads to lower staff turnover and less time off sick. A survey of two thousand employees in the UK found that 62 percent of those who engaged in fun activities at work had taken no sick days in the last three months.[12] When your employees enjoy improved physical and mental health, they're going to perform better. They'll be happier personally and professionally, have higher levels of energy, and embrace the right mental outlook to tackle whatever workplace challenges come their way.

PLAY Amplifies and Extends the Benefits of Exercise

Finding opportunities to get your workforce more physically active will provide physical and mental health benefits to your team that benefit your organization as well. *And when you add the element of play to group activities, you effectively multiply the benefits.*

Providing an opportunity for your employees to play together doesn't need to be complicated or costly. Sign up a team for an adult recreational sports league in whatever city (or cities) your staff are working in and cover the cost for them. Provide company jerseys (for an extra marketing

---

[12]   Paul Harris, "Why it Pays to Play: Workplace Fun Breeds Employee Wellbeing and Productivity," *HR Magazine,* April 12, 2016, https://www.hrmagazine.co.uk/content/other/why-it-pays-to-play -workplace-fun-breeds-employee-wellbeing-and-productivity.

boost) and watch the friendships and bonds develop—between your marketing, finance, and HR teams—that may otherwise never have happened. For approximately $6–10/week per employee, the value that both your staff personally and your organization overall will derive from playful physical activity will be priceless. Research shows that when regular opportunities for physical play are created, your employees will do the following:[13]

- Feel happier and less stressed, due to the endorphins released

- Experience improved cognitive health

- Lower their risk of developing dementia and other age-related conditions

- Feel less lonely or isolated and thus more empowered to ward off depression

- Be more alert and energetic

---

[13] Lawrence Robinson, et al., "The Benefits of Play for Adults," Help Guide, July 2021, https://www.helpguide.org/articles/mental-health/benefits-of-play-for-adults.htm#:~:text=Play%20helps%3A&text=Endorphins%20promote%20an%20overall%20sense,problems%20and%20improve%20brain%20function.

- Expand their creativity

- Be more fit, both mentally and physically

I want to stress that any kind of exercise is better than none. But if you can integrate exercise with a social outlet by playing a team sport—like soccer, beach volleyball, softball, or tennis—where physical activity and social connections combine, you will enjoy greater mental health benefits while feeling happier and adding years to your life.

If you want to get your work team in the game and playing some adult rec sports, go to kristiherold.com/resources for a list of leagues around North America that our JAM team would endorse.

Softball Slim

I recently spoke with a player in our leagues,[14] James Renwick, who goes by the nickname "Softball Slim," and I learned that he lost over one hundred pounds thanks in large part to joining JAM's sports leagues. To watch the interview with Softball Slim go to kristiherold.com/resources.

---

[14] Sportsocialclub "Member Moment—Weight Loss—Softball Slim," YouTube video, 9:01, June 12, 2019, watch video at kristiherold.com/resources.

Feeling that he needed to get active and having a desire to play sports and connect with others, James signed up for a softball league. He explained, "Knowing that I had to get out and play every week helped inspire me to lose weight and live a healthier lifestyle."

Playing team sports in a recreational setting with a strong social component motivated James to take steps to improve his physical health. Having fun playing with other people gave him the incentive to exercise and lose weight. Making the commitment to be on a team helped him stay accountable; after all, if he didn't show up to play, he'd be letting his team down. Taking part in team sports helped Softball Slim stay dedicated to his exercise goals while playing a fun game with a group of people who quickly became good friends.

Social Connectivity Can Lead to Better Mental Health Outcomes

Have you heard of the Blue Zones? They refer to five regions around the world that have been studied and identified as the areas with the largest percentage of individuals one hundred years of age or older. They include parts of California, Costa Rica, Italy, Greece, and Japan.

BLUE ZONES

People in these Blue Zone communities tend to live significantly longer, happier, and healthier lives. All these regions share key characteristics and lifestyle habits such as consuming a plant-heavy diet and *prioritizing tight-knit social networks*. The fact that the Blue Zones all prioritize socialization and community also backs up the Mayo Clinic studies, which show that combining play and socialization with your exercise will add to your longevity.

I am fortunate to be part of a very special community of global entrepreneurs called MMT, which was founded by my innovative friend Jayson Gaignard in 2013. Jayson has worked hard over the years to curate a community of wise, generous, and fun-loving entrepreneurs, who meet regularly in the spirit of learning and growing both personally and professionally.

We typically meet a few times throughout the year for smaller group dinners, speaking events, and shared experiences. And once a year Jayson and his amazing team organize a large conference gathering, where together we attend workshops and seminars, listen to inspiring speakers, and participate in group exercise like hikes, mountain biking, and kayaking. There is always an element of play at these events, which really helps everyone to get to know each other better and strengthen trust among the community.

In 2019, Adam Franklin, a fellow MMTer and the president of Franklin Sports, organized a fun "Buckets Challenge" during the conference. Adam had us sign up, and then he put us in teams of two in order to play for a $10,000 grand prize that Franklin Sports was generously donating to the winning team's charities of choice. I was partnered with Ben Greenfield, another MMTer, which felt incredibly intimidating. I didn't know Ben well at all, but I did know he was an uber athlete, having competed at a world class level in many Ironmans, played multiple varsity sports in college, and competed as a professional obstacle course racer. Ben had been voted America's Top Professional Trainer, named to the Top 100 Most Influential People in Health and Fitness, and graced the cover of *Outside* magazine. So as you can imagine, suddenly being partnered with Ben for a competition felt intense—actually minorly terrifying—even though we were only playing Buckets (effectively a larger scale and family-friendly game of beer pong played with tennis balls and water).

Kristi Herold, Ben Greenfield, Jayson Gaignard and Adam Franklin.

Suffice to say, while there was minimal physical training needed or involved, Ben and I did use some visualization techniques throughout the event. I managed to hold my own and together we won the Buckets championship—and we each got to donate $5,000 to our charity of choice.

After the tournament was over, I reflected on how my relationship with Ben had changed so quickly. Having that couple of hours playing together allowed us to get to know each other better personally. The guy who had felt so intimidating to me a few hours earlier was now a friend—just a regular human who liked to play and laugh like I did. Having said that, it's unlikely I'll be asking Ben to join me for a bike ride or a run anytime soon!

The MMT community works and plays together, and there is a generosity, vulnerability, and trust among this group that is rare and powerful. I feel like I could call any one of this group at any time to ask for help, and they would be there for me. And conversely, I would bend over backward to help any one of them in need if I were able to do so. So as studies on the Blue Zones have proven, play and strong social communities are incredibly beneficial for our mental health and wellness.

"Your Leagues Literally Saved My Life"

About five years ago, I received an email that brought tears to my eyes and incredible joy to my heart. It was from a woman whom I will call Erin and who was a soccer player in our leagues. Erin shared with us that when she first moved to Toronto, she didn't know anyone in the city and found herself struggling with both loneliness and depression. A coworker from her office invited her to play soccer on a company team in our JAM leagues. Figuring she had nothing to lose, Erin decided to give it a try.

Erin ended up having so much fun and loved playing soccer in the league. Joining a recreational league was a major turning point for her, helping her find friends to engage with and lifting her out of loneliness and depression. In her email message to our team, she wrote, "I want to thank JAM for the work you do getting people playing recreational sports. I want you to know that *your leagues literally saved my life.*" This story truly shows how powerful the mental health benefits of play can be.

They Got Our Logo Tattooed on Their Body

Mari Wager has multiple sclerosis (MS). They are an incredible individual who doesn't let their illness hold them back. In 2017, they signed up to play with us across four different sports: volleyball, kickball, ultimate, and basketball. Mari shared with us that our leagues have changed their life.[15] To watch our interview with Mari, go to kristiherold.com/resources.

They explained that sometimes their MS flares up to the point that they can't be physically active. "I play when I can," they said, "but when I'm unable to, I still go out to the games using my walker or cane and stand or sit on the sidelines to cheer my team on and socialize with everyone. After the games we all go out for a beer together."

Even when their MS won't allow them to play sports, they still feel a part of the community as they engage socially with their league friends. This level of engagement provides them with incredible mental health benefits. Mari told us that because of how our leagues transformed them, they decided to become a player for life and get a tattoo of our logo.

I feel so honored that Mari would get our logo tattooed on their body because of the positive impact the socialization

---

[15] Sportsocialclub, "Member Moment—Monday Member—Adam," YouTube video 0:50, September 25, 2019, watch video at kristiherold.com/resources.

of playing in our leagues has made on their life. In fact, Mari is not alone; we've had four different players get a tattoo of our logo because of how playing in the leagues has benefited each of their lives in such powerful ways. Clearly, our JAM team's commitment to connecting people through play is making a powerful, positive impact on both people's physical and mental health. It is truly humbling to witness and be part of these extraordinary transformations.

PLAYful Physical Activity
Can Significantly Decrease Stress

One big foe constantly being battled in our North American workforce is stress. Stress exists everywhere you look and can have many sources:

- Customer demands

- Deadline pressures

- Worries about job performance or fear of job loss

- Workplace disagreements

- Being overworked

- Feeling invisible, voiceless, or overlooked

Here's where play at work can help. Opportunities to play can ease the tension created by workplace stressors. Workplace playtime that combines social interactions, physical activity, and an element of fun can greatly reduce the stress that many employees are feeling.

Fun physical activity and time spent playing help to decrease stress by triggering an increase in dopamine—a neurotransmitter that allows us to feel pleasure—and a decrease in cortisol, which is the hormone responsible for stress.

> If you're tired of seeing your employees stressed and burnt out, do yourself (and them) a favor and create opportunities for playful physical activities at your workplace.

The health benefits your employees will enjoy from playful activities will help them individually with improved physical and mental health and will also benefit your entire organization. A physically and mentally healthy work team will have less absences and be more productive and better able to work together to develop innovative ideas to help your company rise to the top.

Leading a Business at Age 101

Recently, I had the incredible opportunity to have a phone call with an amazing man named Brit Smith, who at the age of 101 is still leading the company he founded in 1954, sixty-eight years ago. Homestead Land Holdings Ltd. is a real estate company with almost nine hundred employees that has grown to be one of Canada's largest and most respected landlord companies.

Before I spoke to Brit, I did a little research on him and was blown away and completely humbled by what I learned. Born in 1920, Brit served in WWII, later became a lawyer, and then went on to start his real estate business at the age of thirty-three. Over the last one hundred years, he has been recognized for his incredible philanthropic efforts and community service with multiple accolades, including the esteemed Order of Canada which he received in 2019.

I learned about Brit through his granddaughter, who sits on the board of their family business. When I asked her what the secrets to Brit's sharpness and longevity are, she told me, "He naps every day, and he is playful." Hearing him described as "playful" of course made me want to learn more—so I asked her for an introduction.

What I most loved about getting to meet Brit was learning more about how he plays! He told me that he played tennis until just a few years ago, finally hanging up his racket at the age of ninety-five, and that he plays the crossword puzzle in the newspaper every day.

Brit told me that he believes people are absolutely critical when growing a business. You need to have people who are keen to find better ways to do things and who enjoy having fun at work. As Brit said, "a certain amount of levity is essential in life."

Francine Moore was hired in 1997 as Brit's CFO, and when I spoke with her, she recalled that Brit was so much fun during her first interview that she giggled her way through it. Francine has now been working with Homestead for twenty-five years and has since become president. As she shared with me, "Brit truly is playful, he can laugh at himself, and it filters down throughout the organization." Francine shared memories of corporate boat cruises with over 150 of their staff and playing games like "Minute to Win It." As she explained, "Gathering people who may not typically work together to laugh and play at events like this really helps strengthen our corporate culture, one in which we truly value humor and playfulness."

I chatted with Brit about a variety of ways his team has incorporated play in the workplace while also giving back to the community, all of which I found incredibly inspiring. He shared about how they will get groups of twelve to twenty people from their office to paddle together in a war canoe, or ride on a fifteen-seater bicycle around town, wearing T-shirts with the company logo on them, all to raise money and awareness for charities they support. As Brit said, "Bicycle riding or boat paddling is not what is important, but rather having fun together as a team, working in unison, and learning to literally pull together."

Given that I'm about halfway to Brit's age, I'm excited to use my next fifty-one years wisely. I feel inspired to continue being playful myself, while working to positively impact lives of others by connecting people through play and giving back to our communities. I am also inspired to make more time for naps!

PLAYful Physical Activity Releases
Feel-Good Hormones

According to Darryl Edwards,[16] health advocate and creator of the Primal Play Method™, people can boost their happy hormones through play.

Darryl reminds us of the chemical and biological reasons that playing makes you feel better. The feel-good hormones that are released with even just thirty minutes of play can reduce the stress you're feeling and make a world of difference to your mental health.

These are the feel-good hormones that are released when you play:

- *Endorphins*: They help you feel more positive and energized while improving your immune response and reducing stress

- *Oxytocin*: Activities that create bonds between people lead to a release of this "hug hormone," which can help build trusting, stable relationships

[16] Darryl Edwards, "Play and The Feel Good Hormone." Primal Play, June 23, 2016, https://www.primalplay.com/blog/play-and-the-feel -good-hormones.

- *Dopamine*: Any form of play can release dopamine, which helps people feel happier and increases their ability to focus and learn

- *Serotonin*: This hormone protects you against depression while helping you sleep better and handle stress

If you want to ensure that you and your teammates get the benefit of all these amazing hormones, then keep playing!

My Own Experience with Individual and Team Sports

Growing up, my main sport was alpine ski racing. I was an individual athlete, competing against other individuals, as opposed to being a team sport athlete. Having said that, we always traveled and trained as a team, so I did enjoy many of the benefits of being part of a team, even while competing individually. I was always surrounded by supportive teammates who were close friends as we traveled and competed around the world.

Those teammates were like my brothers and sisters. To this day I enjoy strong bonds with them. So in many cases, an individual sport can *become* a team sport, offering the social connections that release oxytocin and dopamine, as well as the physical activity that releases serotonin and endorphins.

My personal experience tells me that it doesn't matter so much whether you're engaged in an individual activity or a group one. What matters most is having these elements present in some way:

- Physical activity

- Social connection

- Measure of fun

I loved being a competitive skier and traveling with my team. Outside of skiing I also gravitated toward team sports. In high school, I signed up for every team sport I could, including basketball, volleyball, and flag football.

After university, as a small-town girl (I am from Sudbury, Ontario), I moved to the big city of Toronto and didn't know a lot of people there. Looking to meet people and make new friends, I was introduced to the self-officiated sport of Ultimate Frisbee. Playing Ultimate opened my eyes to just how easy it is to meet other like-minded people while playing team sports, enjoying social interactions, staying active, and having some fun.

In fact, playing Ultimate gave me the inspiration to start my business running adult recreational sports leagues. Forming friendships with people while playing team sports was such a powerful experience that I wanted to help create these types of opportunities for other people as well, and not just in Toronto but in many regions across Canada and the United States.

Meeting Their Loves and Best Friends

At JAM, we have heard thousands of stories of people meeting the loves of their lives or their best friends by playing in our leagues.

One story started with an email I received from a player many years ago:

> Hi Kristi, I just wanted to pass along a note of thanks. I have been playing basketball with JAM for many years. Three years ago, I signed up for an individual basketball team, as did Scott, and last month we got married. I wanted to thank you for running such a great league, where not only can you meet

wonderful people, but also have a ball of fun. Thanks for playing a part in our fate!

Annette

Recently, Annette shared a post on social media celebrating her fifteenth anniversary with Scott: *"It all started with a singles game of basketball with JAM, and 15 years, 3 kids and one pup later and we are still having a ball!"*

Annette and Scott—wedding day.

Annette, Scott and family.

Perhaps one of my favorites of our JAM love stories is this one from a player in our leagues back in 1998, Rob Davies:

> For years, we played against each other in the Wednesday night indoor gym soccer league. At the time, I only knew her as the "woman in the yellow socks." In conversation with her team captain, I discovered that my attraction to her was mutual. Our separate teams would often end up at the same bar post-game,

so I got to know her both on and off the court, and we made a lasting connection. Within a few years, we were married AND had joined forces on the soccer field.

The reason Rob's story is one of my favorites is that shortly after Rob met the love of his life playing in our leagues, he also saw an announcement that we were looking to hire an employee. Rob applied for the job and was hired as one of our earliest employees. He has since become a partner in the business, and we've been working side by side now connecting people through play for over twenty-two years. I also happen to know that Rob has remained close friends with many of the teammates he first met playing in our leagues over two decades ago.

These stories and so many others illustrate the powerful mental health benefits from the social connections that form when we play together. People bond and form strong friendships. Sometimes they even fall in love.

From Levi Cooperman, Founder of FreshBooks

Have you heard of FreshBooks? This massively successful company helps small business owners and freelancers by providing a convenient solution that streamlines invoicing, payments, and financial reporting. What started as a tiny operation now employs over five hundred people around the world.

Levi Cooperman, a co-founder of FreshBooks and professional engineer, met the love of his life, Naama, through JAM's play opportunities. Here's his story, in his own words:

It was the summer of 2003 when Naama and I first started playing Ultimate Frisbee together with JAM. We had met playing baseball a number of years prior to that, but it was really the team with JAM that sparked our relationship.

I believe it was a Tuesday or Thursday night team, and I think it was one of the first iterations of our team called Banana Cream Pie. I invited Naama out to play and I don't think she had played Ultimate before then.

We obviously hit it off on the field and, of course, even more so when socializing at the pubs over nachos and beers after the games. We started dating that fall and were never apart from that point forward. We got married in the summer of 2007 and now have a family of four. I've always been a loyal member and a big fan of JAM!

FreshBooks, the organization Levi is a cofounder of, cares deeply about its culture and its people. They have been recognized with many awards over the years, including making the prestigious "Canada's Top 100 Employers" list, being certified as a Great Place to Work—Canada, and being named to "Greater Toronto's Top Employers" list.[17] Over the last decade or so, FreshBooks has had many different company teams playing in our JAM sports leagues across a variety of sports, including dodgeball, floor hockey, and softball. Over the last couple of years, FreshBooks has also participated in quite a number of virtual team-bonding events hosted by JAM. This small commitment to providing a playful opportunity for human connection between its colleagues has helped FreshBooks strengthen its culture while employees forge stronger friendships both inside and outside the office.

---

[17] "The Global Authority on Workplace Culture," Great Place to Work, 2022, https://www.greatplacetowork.ca/en/.

Levi Cooperman and family.

It's amazing what play can do. Friendships and romantic relationships blossom and stronger teams get built at the office when coworkers play together. The benefits of these relationships can be felt across the board, from the senior leaders to the newest employees. When people form strong relationships, the mental health boost is phenomenal, and it carries over into every aspect of life, including work.

To read more stories about love connections that were created through play go to kristiherold.com/resources.

Here's What Healthier, Happier Employees Look Like

Do you want a happier, healthier workplace? Of course, you do. Happier employees are more productive, energetic, and positive. With happier employees, conflicts are fewer, customers get better service, and your organization performs better.

Many organizations will sponsor their employees to sign up corporate teams to play in adult recreational sports leagues, across a wide variety of sports. Companies that provide this playful outlet to their employees get the benefits of having these happier, healthier employees working for them as well as the stronger bonds between their employees that have formed from playing together. Not only that, but there's the marketing benefit of having a team of employees wearing their company's name on their sports jerseys out on the soccer field or kickball diamond.

With opportunities to play in place, you'll have a happier and healthier group of employees who value what you're doing for them and appreciate the chance to play and make important friendship connections. Your employees will feel personally cared for by you as their employer.

From Bruce Poon Tip, Founder of G Adventures

A pioneer in community tourism, Bruce Poon Tip founded G Adventures, which grew to having over three thousand full-time employees and one thousand travel guides pre-pandemic. The small group adventure travel company has been transforming the travel landscape. Operating for over thirty years, G Adventures strives to give travelers a more authentic experience by connecting them with locals during their trips. Bruce believes in investing heavily in his people for their physical and mental well-being, and his company culture celebrates happiness and freedom.

Bruce firmly believes there is power in all types of play. For many years (pre-pandemic), G Adventures always had five to seven sports offerings available at any given time for their staff. Many were teams playing in a variety of sports with JAM. There was also a dragon boat racing team and teams in mud run and obstacle race (OCR)–type experiences.

As Bruce says, "There is no single better way to unite a company team toward a common goal than to compete through sports together." I couldn't agree more.

It Doesn't Have to Be Just Sports

I want to take a moment to emphasize that, as fun and rewarding as recreational sports can be, play isn't limited just to sports. There are infinite ways to have fun and engage socially with others while enjoying physical and mental health benefits.

Playing can involve music, for example. I know of companies that have their own bands, complete with rehearsals and periodic concerts.

Theater is another great form of play. I helped to start an adult community musical theater group over a decade ago, and our troupe has done over eleven performances together over the years, raising over half a million dollars for charity in the process. Playing on stage together as we rehearse our singing, dancing, and acting is a great social outlet that has incredible physical and mental health benefits.

While we started the theater troupe back in 2009, if you talk with anyone in my cast today, they'll tell you that some of their very best friends are from this group. Again, it's all about the bonds and social connections that form when adults make time to play together.

If sports work for your organization, that is great. But if not, remember that you can create other healthy ways to play and have your workplace teams benefit from them. Musical theater, improv or comedy classes, talent shows, book clubs, karaoke nights, escape rooms, playing in a band, dancing, lunchtime board games or puzzles…it's all play, and it's all good!

A Crisis That Needs to Be Addressed

Even before the pandemic, North America had reached a real crisis with the following:

- Obesity

- Anxiety

- Depression

- Loneliness

Obesity

Obesity is a medical condition characterized by having too much body fat, which can cause health problems and complications. Over the last twenty-five years (pre-pandemic) obesity rates across North America had been on the rise among adults and children. The age-adjusted prevalence of obesity in adults from 2017–2018 was 42.4 percent, according to the Centers for Disease Control and Prevention in 2020.

OBESITY RATES CONTINUE TO TREND UP IN U.S.

Percentage of U.S. adults who are obese based on height and weight survey

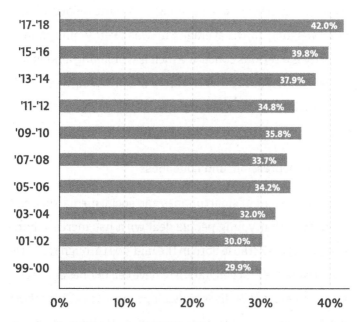

Year	Percentage
'17-'18	42.0%
'15-'16	39.8%
'13-'14	37.9%
'11-'12	34.8%
'09-'10	35.8%
'07-'08	33.7%
'05-'06	34.2%
'03-'04	32.0%
'01-'02	30.0%
'99-'00	29.9%

Data collected by CDC based on survey of 5,000 U.S. adults.
Source: Centers for Disease Control and Prevention

Statistics from a Harvard study in 2020 show that on average, one out of every three adults is obese, which is about 36 percent of the population. And based on information from the Centers for Disease Control and Prevention in 2019, about 18.5 percent of children ages two to nineteen are considered obese in the United States.

And concerningly, for many people, the pandemic escalated this already serious issue. According to a Harris Poll, 42 percent of respondents had experienced undesired weight gain during the pandemic. Among those who reported undesired weight gain, the average gain was twenty-nine pounds. Obesity is a serious concern which is worsening among our society and leads to other health issues including heart problems, diabetes, stress, and more.

Anxiety, Depression, and Loneliness

With the advent of smartphones and social media, the level of anxiety that young people deal with has increased dramatically. Gen Z (those born in the mid '90s through the early 2010s) were the first generation to have cell phones and social media access in their lives at much younger ages. This cohort has been shown to experience significantly higher levels of anxiety and depression compared to people born before 1995. According to the American Psychological Association,[18] just 45 percent of Gen Zers report that their mental health is very good or excellent. All other generation groups fared better

---

[18]   Sophie Bethune, "Gen Z More Likely to Report Mental Health Concerns," American Psychological Association, January 2019, https://www.apa.org /monitor/2019/01/gen-z.

on this statistic, including millennials (56 percent), Gen Xers (51 percent), and boomers (70 percent).

Paradoxically, while Gen Z has grown up in a hyper-concentrated social media world, they report feeling far lonelier than older demographic groups.

GEN Z IS LONELY
Percent of U.S. adults who are lonely, shown as demographics

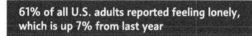

61% of all U.S. adults reported feeling lonely, which is up 7% from last year

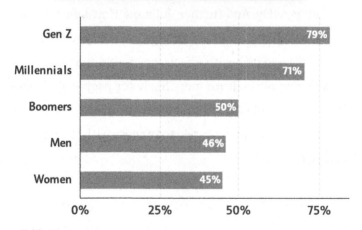

n=10,441 adults
Survey was conducted during the summer of 2019.
Source: Ipsos Polling for Cigna U.S. Loneliness Index

Hyper-connectivity with our digital devices seems to have evoked intense feelings of isolation and loneliness. The 24/7 stream of negative news combined with a fear of missing out (FOMO) and constant comparisons to others on social media has ignited hopelessness, shame, exhaustion, and depression.

Greater Social Connection Is Associated with 50 Percent Lower Odds of Early Death

According to Douglas Nemecek, MD,[19] Cigna's chief medical officer for behavioral health, the negative effects of loneliness on our health are equivalent to smoking fifteen cigarettes a day. And further, Julianne Holt-Lunstad, PhD, a psychologist at Brigham Young University who studies loneliness and its health effects, has found that loneliness makes premature death more likely for people of all ages. One of her studies found that lonely people are 50 percent more likely to die prematurely than those with strong social connections.

In all these areas, we as a society were in full crisis mode before COVID-19, and the pandemic has only worsened the

[19] Nick Tate, "Loneliness Rivals Obesity, Smoking as Health Risk," WebMD, May 4, 2018, https://www.webmd.com/balance/news/20180504/loneliness -rivals-obesity-smoking-as-health-risk.

situation. It is imperative that people everywhere, including business leaders, take the necessary steps to do what we can to help improve the mental and physical health of ourselves and our employees. Given that any kind of play can have real mental health benefits, and getting active brings about physical health benefits, businesses of all sizes can do their part to help bring us out of this crisis by making play an integral part of their business model.

A Solution for the New Hybrid and Remote Paradigms

The benefits of play are not new; however, the pandemic definitely amplified the issues being faced by so many in our society in regard to loneliness, anxiety, and depression, when the inability to socially connect in person with others was mandated. Further, as a majority of offices around the world moved to a remote work model, and with many deciding to stay remote or hybrid after mandates lifted, the need for work colleagues to find ways to connect playfully has become more and more apparent.

As we emerge from the pandemic, some companies are going back to the in-person, in-office work model. Many others are giving their employees the option to continue working remotely. And a lot of companies are adopting a hybrid approach, with some employees at the office two or three days a week and working from home on other days.

When work hours and locations become so varied, the constant that unites everyone can be *play*. It's the perfect way to restore that missing human connection, and it can be easily incorporated in a variety of ways for in-person, hybrid, or fully remote teams.

Having a weekly recreation gathering point for people in the same city who don't see each other in the office anymore is a great solution. What brings them together can be sports, music, theater, dance, or any other form of play that has a strong social component. For organizations that are spread across multiple cities—or whose employees perhaps moved away from the city where the office is during the pandemic and are now going to be working remotely—there is still the ability to connect for some virtual fun and play. Many organizations like JAM can provide turnkey fun connections like escape rooms, scavenger hunts, and game shows to help hybrid or remote teams stay connected, laughing and playing together. And from a practical perspective, play will also help your employer-provided health insurance program. That's because, having created opportunities for your team to physically or virtually play and laugh, they will be a happier and healthier group and thus far less likely to need medical assistance and/or to call in sick.

As most work teammates will now likely see less of each other in-person at the office, having the opportunity to gather weekly or monthly for physical play of sports, music, etc. for some virtual laughs feels more essential than ever.

For more resources on turnkey offerings to get your team playing virtually, in-person, or in a hybrid format, go to kristiherold.com/resources.

Chapter 3 Key Takeaway Points

→ Forms of play that blend physical activity and fun with social interactions can do wonders for an employee's physical and mental health

→ Social play amplifies the benefits of exercise, leading to greater mental and physical fitness and less anxiety, stress, depression, and loneliness

→ Physical health benefits of play can come from sports, theater, music, dance, and countless other fun group activities

→ Mental health benefits of play can come from all of the above, as well as just connecting virtually for some laugh-filled play

→ Workers who have improved their mental and physical health will call in sick less often and perform better at work

Not only do workplace team sports and group activities play an important role in keeping people physically and mentally healthy, but playing together also improves the energy of your team.

PLAY Improves Energy

*"When you're following your energy and
doing what you want all the time, the distinction
between work and play dissolves."*

—SHAKTI GAWAIN

Did you know that according to a Hartford 2021 survey, 61 percent of employees are burned out at their jobs?[20]

---

[20] The Hartford Staff, "Majority of US Workers Experiencing Burnout at Work," *The Hartford*, March 5, 2021, https://www.thehartford.com /insights/future-of-benefits/occupational-burnout-survey.

You know what burnout feels like. It zaps your energy. It makes you numb. Burnout also comes with physical fatigue that's hard to overcome. You feel tired and your brain gets fuzzy, making it hard to concentrate and do your job well.

Having to drag yourself to work every day can be extremely stressful if you're feeling burned out, and stress can lead to all kinds of ailments. A report from UMass Lowell estimates that stress costs businesses an estimated $200 to $300 billion a year in health costs, absenteeism, and poor performance or lost productivity. The report also says that 40 percent of turnover is due to stress, and we know how costly turnover is (having discussed that in Chapter 1). These are massive financial losses that can be reduced and avoided by taking the importance of play and fun more seriously.

COST OF DOING NOTHING

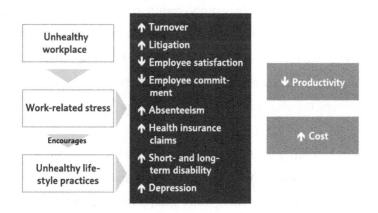

We know that play reduces stress, so it stands to reason that investing in workplace opportunities for play can lower the incidence of stress-related illnesses and, in turn, put a stop to so much lost productivity and wasted resources.

More than a Dusty Ping-Pong Table

For years now, many companies have realized that, far from distracting their employees or making them less productive, a Ping-Pong table in the office can in fact help energize people and make them more productive.

It doesn't have to be just Ping-Pong; there could be a pool table at the office. Or puzzles or Nerf balls to toss around. Anything that invites play and creates opportunities for fun human connection away from a spreadsheet or boardroom table will improve the energy of your team. That's why you see these types of recreational items frequently at businesses, especially in newer organizations.

But having a Ping-Pong table in the office just as a cool piece of decor, a way to outwardly signal that an organization has a fun culture, is nothing more than posturing. In contrast, a Ping-Pong table that is well-used with weekly full-staff games of "around the world"—or singles and doubles ladder matches getting played over the course of a month—will add real energy to your team. The laughter that you'll hear throughout your office during those games will be a far truer sign of a fun, healthy culture than the table itself. After playing together for a few minutes, your team will be more prepared to face work challenges head-on when they return to their desks reenergized.

If you have play areas at work (and good for you if you do), you must also foster an environment where play among coworkers is encouraged. Your pool tables and Ping-Pong tables, your company gyms, your indoor bikes and trikes

…they're *not* props. They are tools to energize people and strengthen your culture—use them!

And while these tools are good, they're not enough. You need an even greater emphasis on play if you really want to energize your workers.

Beyond Your
Company Building

A strong work culture actually extends beyond your company office building (or in this new remote and hybrid world, beyond a traditional workday). This means you need to create opportunities for play outside of the office *and* nine to five. In larger organizations, people from different divisions may in fact never meet each other because their jobs don't intersect. Providing opportunities for people to meet and play outside of their day-to-day life—perhaps by offering a variety of recreational sports teams for people to sign up for or a fun virtual escape room or trivia league—will help improve your culture. These are easy-to-implement and low-cost investments that will yield high returns, as people from different departments will meet each other and become friends, simply by playing in different types of activities together.

Any playful pursuits that your employees engage in together present possibilities for greater connections between your separate departments or divisions. And this brings a strong unifying force that will breathe new life and energy into your organization. As team sports and group activities bring together individuals from different areas of the business, not only will you see stronger friendships but also an appreciation and respect for what each member does and the unique contributions they bring to the organization.

Learning to Win and Lose as a Team

In the previous chapter I mentioned Bruce Poon Tip, founder of G Adventures, and his belief that the most powerful way to unite a team toward a common goal is by competing through sports together. In addition to uniting people, playing team sports simply *energizes* everyone. Science has proven time and again across a huge variety of studies that "movement is medicine."

Bruce is also a believer in the importance of learning the art of winning and losing. When people are playing together and competing toward a goal, some will win and some will lose, but all can have fun. Celebrating wins is fantastic, and it's something that G Adventures does really well.

For example, Bruce explained, at their annual conference they have the G World Cup, and the winning team receives a trophy that's "so massive they have to break it down and pack pieces into their suitcases to bring it home." A desire to win can energize employees to be hungry for success, something that carries over into their jobs and the goals of the business very nicely.

But winning isn't everything, and Bruce makes it a point to focus on the art of losing as well as winning. He believes it's important to know how to lose. When people lose together, there's a lot of learning to be gained from that experience.

While winning is certainly fun and energizing, losing provides teachable moments and opportunities for growth. Both are necessary to move forward in life and in the workplace.

Losing as a team creates opportunities for the following:

- Asking and exploring what could have been done better

- Learning and opening up new ways of doing things

- Strategizing how to do better next time

- Getting energized and excited about the chance to try again

Do you see how this can carry over beautifully into the workplace? Both winning and losing can be energizing, and in addition, knowing how to embrace the art of losing can have benefits in all areas of life, including work.

I have always encouraged my team to "find a better way" (one of our core values at JAM), even if mistakes are made as we try. I remind them it is okay and expected that we will all make mistakes along the way. The key is not to repeat them but rather to learn and grow from them. That, too, is part of the art of losing well.

Benefiting Together Regardless

So win or lose, everyone benefits. Wins are celebrated. Losses are learned from. In the end, everyone's in it together. Everyone's in it for fun. Everybody wants to feel energized.

Participating in physically intense competitions like a mud run or OCR-style events push people to reach higher and do better than they ever thought they could. But in order to succeed, the focus must be on teamwork. Bruce and his G

Adventures colleagues have competed in events like this, and what he loves about them is not just the way they build participants' confidence to crush every obstacle in their paths, but how they also foster a spirit of leaving no one behind. Teams do everything in their power to get across the finish line together.

Having friendly competitions creates opportunities to celebrate all types of wins, from individual triumphs to company-wide successes. These competitions also lead to opportunities for coming together, strategizing, and learning from losses. Through it all, the common thread that unites and energizes everyone is camaraderie and teamwork.

I don't think any workplace meeting, no matter how interesting it may be, can accomplish this. I believe play is a far better tool for building camaraderie and learning to work together as a team toward a shared goal and purpose. *Playing together also creates fantastic opportunities for connections and positive synergies to form between employees from different divisions of your organization.*

Bring Outside Inspiration Back to Work

Giving employees permission to play is an incredible way to get them inspired. When we are inspired by something, we feel energized—whether it's from a new idea, a new experience, or anything looked at from a fresh new angle. Playful activities can inspire, leading us to feel revived.

Bruce from G Adventures told me he doesn't want his people working at the office all the time. He wants them to go out and enjoy new, playful experiences where they can find renewed inspiration in life. Whether it's wine tasting, soccer, or music, he wants his employees to be experiencing life and really living. As Bruce said, "It is these lived experiences that they will get their inspiration from that they ultimately bring back with them to work."

If you're just sitting at your desk all the time, nothing new is going to happen, and you'll feel stuck in stagnant energy. New experiences breathe new life and energy into the workplace.

On a related note, at JAM, we don't believe in sitting in the office for long, long hours trying to look busy. We believe in getting our jobs done as efficiently as possible—in fact, one of our other core values is "get shit done." We also believe in the restorative power of taking small breaks throughout the day to boost our energy.

Mini Breaks Are Like Mini Vacations

One of the things we like to encourage at JAM is for people to get away from their desks at lunchtime. Instead of sitting at our desks eating lunch and surfing the net, we encourage our team to eat together—to either head to the lunchroom or hop on a Zoom to enjoy some laughs over lunch with our colleagues. We also encourage our team to use this time midday to head outside for fresh air or get a workout in. In my experience, getting away from your desk results in a huge energy boost.

Studies have shown that breaks throughout the day and detaching from work helps to increase levels of energy and reduce exhaustion.[21] Further, these mini breaks are like mini vacations, as they refresh your mind, restore your spirits, and reenergize you, enabling you to get back to work with a fresh, new perspective.

[21] Marjaana Sianoja, et al., "Recovery during Lunch Breaks: Testing Long-Term Relations with Energy Levels at Work," *Scandinavian Journal of Work and Organizational Psychology*, August 30, 2016, https://www.sjwop.com/articles/10.16993/sjwop.13/.

About a month ago, I found myself working away, with tons to do, when I noticed on my calendar that I had a virtual escape room event coming up in a few minutes. In the midst of being consumed by the tasks at hand, I thought to myself, *I don't have time for this!*

I debated not going. But then I stopped myself. I told myself that no matter how busy I was, I would go to this social event. As the CEO of the company, I should be at the event. It's my opportunity to connect with different people at different levels, something I value immensely.

So despite being swamped with work, I attended the virtual social event. And you know what? It did me a world of good! Just minutes into the event, I found myself very much in the moment, laughing and playing with my team. When that hour was done, I could not believe how much better I felt. During that virtual escape room experience I met some people who I didn't work with regularly and got to know them on a more personal level.

Taking this time to play boosted my energy, enabling me to get back to what I was doing and work far more efficiently and productively than I had been before I took the break to enjoy the event.

Stop Being Stuck in the Work, Work, Work Mentality

I feel that society in general has the idea that to get ahead, you have to work like a maniac. Just keep working. Work harder. Work more. Work, work, work, and work some more.

Often, I am guilty of having this mentality just as much as anyone else. But the problem with this mindset is that constant work without breaks or moments of play leads to burnout. This gives rise to stress-related illnesses that cost companies billions in lost productivity. Burnout is a destroyer of great employees.

The push-yourself-to-work-even-harder mentality is based on the false notion that working nonstop will get us to our goals faster. The reality is that working nonstop will probably get us closer to a mental or physical breakdown.

It may sound counterintuitive, but to perform your best and work more efficiently, you need to take the time to play.

It's time to get unstuck. If you're an employee, give yourself a break and some necessary playtime. If you're an employer, give your people the gift of play opportunities. It's a gift that will come back to you in the form of a happier, more energized, and more productive workforce.

One day recently, I had so much on my plate. I sat at my desk and worked and worked and worked all day long. After dinner, I worked more. Before I knew it, it was ten o'clock at night, and besides my dinner break I had been working straight through since 8:00 a.m. My to-do list seemed never-ending. I had worked so hard, and yet there was still so much more to do (as there always will be). I was drained.

The very next night, I decided on a different approach. I closed my computer, deciding not to go back to it after dinner, knowing that all my work would still be waiting for me in the morning. Instead, I took my teenage son out for driving lessons. Because *this* is what life is about. This is where valuable memories get made, not from sitting at my desk checking more off my task list. Now, I often book "playdates" for myself, such as a yoga class or a walk with a friend, right into my daily work calendar in advance of my week getting filled with work meetings. It's a way of ensuring I get up from my desk to take these much-needed and important breaks each day.

Making valuable memories is no different at work. Of course, we must sit through our business meetings and get our important work done. But this is not where our best memories are going to be made.

Your Best Moments and Memories Come from PLAYtime

Our best moments with our work teams will come from the unusual. The playtimes.

A friend of mine, Jonathan Lister, recently left LinkedIn after twelve years as the vice president of several departments. The day Jonathan announced his departure, he shared a post with seven photos on his LinkedIn profile. He reflected on the top three things he felt he and his team accomplished during his time there. He shared about the growth they had been part of with both membership and revenues, yet what he seemed most proud of was the culture he and many others on his team had helped to create. As Jonathan shared, "Most importantly, we created one of the world's best workplace cultures. The people who do the best at LinkedIn have always been compassionate, ambitious, curious, and fun—along with having an incredible ability to deliver."

What made the biggest impression on me from Jonathan's post were the photos he also shared. Five of the seven photos he posted were pictures of him and his teammates dressed up in silly costumes, clearly having some laughs at some playful corporate events. After twelve years working with his fantastic team, some of his favorite memories were from these playful moments with his team, *not* from sitting in meetings. The powerful memories captured in the photos involved camaraderie, laughter, and play.

Playful LinkedIn culture.

Playful LinkedIn culture.

Good memories, whether at home or work, are made when we are laughing and enjoying life.

Great Places to Work Make Time for PLAY

Sadly, most companies do not make time for play. Employees work all day, go home, work the next day, go home, living an endless, tiresome script. This hamster-wheel work cycle with little to no time for fun and play undoubtedly contributed to the Great Resignation. People don't want to live like this.

The companies we read about that are getting nominated and winning awards for being Great Places to Work have all these things in common:

- They're incredibly successful

- They have motivated, energized employees who want to build great careers

- They make time for playful connections with teammates

It's no coincidence that companies recognized for being great places to work are also successful and also invest in providing their people with quality play experiences. It all goes hand in hand. When your employees want to be at your company, they bring in good energy that spreads to others. When they have opportunities to play and connect, they are more productive, and your organization enjoys more success. It's all tied together.

From Ray Minato, Founder & CEO
Of Inertia Design

Speaking of great companies, I want to share with you some great wisdom from Inertia Design's founder, Ray Minato.

Inertia Design's purpose is "making entrepreneurs' dreams come true." Named as one of Canada's esteemed "Great Places to Work" for three years in a row, Inertia Design topped the charts by taking the number-one position for the under-one-hundred-employees group in 2020.

As an engineer, Ray has always had a passion for designing cars, but not just your run-of-the-mill suburban grocery getter. Ray wanted to be part of a team that designed race cars. He pursued his passion, and it took him to some of the top large engineering and design firms in the world. In time he found himself on teams that were getting awards for car designs that were winning prestigious races, including Daytona and LeMans.

Ray worked at successful organizations, enjoyed rapid career growth, reached amazing milestones with his car designs, and was getting plenty of recognition for his achievements. It was everything he thought he wanted. You'd think he was living the dream.

But the sad reality was that he was miserable.

Why? Because the work environment and management team he worked under were toxic and negative. They were draining his energy. Despite working with his passion of designing cars, Ray found himself working in exactly the type of environment he did not want to be in. So he did something about it: he went off on his own.

He Created the Work Culture He Craved

Knowing exactly the type of company culture he did *not* want to work in made it easier for Ray to focus on creating a work culture for his organization that he did want. From the start, he made a commitment to being completely open, honest, and transparent with his customers. As his business grew, this transparency set the stage for internal transparency among his employees.

Having been part of groups like Entrepreneur's Organization (EO) where business owners share experiences, Ray learned more about vision, values, systems, processes, and cultures of well-run organizations.

Inertia Design now has about fifty full-time employees, and, in addition to ensuring his team is engaged with interesting, challenging work, Ray and his leadership team at Inertia Design also know how critical it is for their employees to be engaged with one another as a team. One of the easiest ways they find to do this is by making a little time for play.

Rocket Monkey

I asked Ray about ways he and his team make time for play at work, and he shared a number of stories with me. One that had me laughing out loud was the story of "Rocket Monkey." Inertia's engineers and designers are constantly coming up with creative ideas, and when that creativity gets a little wonky, they all have a good laugh.

Years ago, someone at the company took a stuffed monkey and strapped it to a rocket-like contraption. At lunch he got everyone to go outside, where he launched his creation with a few minor explosives. Since then, Rocket Monkey has semi-regular launches that the team gets excited about. As the monkey rides everything from a watermelon to a toy car, the Inertia team lets down their guards, reverting to a sense of childhood, recess fun. Some launches are more successful than others, but the common denominator in every launch is the shared laughter and energy boost that happens when work teams take some breaks to play.

If you'd like to enjoy a laugh and watch some videos of Rocket Monkey launches in action, go to kristiherold.com/resources.

Rocket Monkey

Giving the Gift of PLAY to Clients

Inertia Design was one of the early adopters of JAM's virtual events in the summer of 2020. The team enjoyed their regular team-bonding sessions led by our JAM hosts so much that they decided JAM events would be a great gift for their corporate clients. Having seen firsthand the energizing effects of play in the workplace for their own team, Inertia has taken it a step further by giving the gift of a JAM event to many of their corporate clients. Inertia was looking for an original gift idea (let's be honest—no one really gets excited about receiving a gift basket filled with shelf-stable sausage, neon-colored olive oil, or stale biscotti) for their clients, and with a JAM event they were giving the gift of an experience, the gift of play, laughter, and human connection.

As it turned out, some of Inertia's clients who received the gift of a JAM experience enjoyed the energizing effect with their teammates so much that they went on to become repeat clients themselves.

Noticing a Boost in Energy

Ray's team also has a dedicated group of about ten who enjoy playing music, so they rehearse together regularly. A couple times a year, this group puts on concerts for the rest of the company, energizing the band members and listeners alike.

Inertia Design band practice.

According to Ray, even if the Inertia Design team cannot play every single day, when they *do* make time for play—whether it's a JAM session, a Rocket Monkey launch, or an Inertia band rehearsal—he sees a noticeable boost in energy across his entire team for days afterward.

This isn't just anecdotal evidence; at Inertia they measure their eNPS (employee Net Promoter Score) regularly. An eNPS of fifty is considered great, while seventy is considered world-class. The eNPS at Inertia Design is regularly seventy-five or higher! The combination of stimulating intellectual work and making time to play surely has a lot to do with these high scores.

Making time for play—whether it be sports, a game of cards over lunch, or playing music together (play comes in many different shapes and sizes)—packs a powerful energizing punch for those who participate.

> NPS (Net Promoter Score) is a widely used market research metric that typically takes the form of a single survey question asking respondents to rate the likelihood that they would recommend a company, product, or a service to a friend or colleague. eNPS (employee Net Promoter Score) is *a way of measuring how your employees feel about working for your company.*

Short PLAY Breaks at Work Will Boost Your Team's Energy

We all know how a typical workday can, and often does, drain the energy out of employees. Counteract this potential burnout by encouraging your teams to take short breaks and have fun with their colleagues. Instead of seeing an energy drain, you'll see energy boosts.

It really doesn't take much to create these boosts. Depending on the activity, five, ten, or fifteen minutes can be enough to make a big difference.

Ideas for boosting energy through short play breaks and lunchtime fun include the following:[22]

- Leave your desk and talk to someone—be curious and ask them about themselves.

- If you're working remotely, jump on Zoom for a weekly "lunch and laugh." Simply eat lunch and chat—no work talk allowed.

- Take a stroll and bring someone along or enjoy a "walk and talk" chat with a friend on the phone while getting in a short walk.

- Play pool or Ping-Pong with others.

- Book a one-hour virtual event for your team, like a game show, escape room, or scavenger hunt.

---

[22] Marjaana Sianoja, et al., "Recovery during Lunch Breaks: Testing Long-Term Relations with Energy Levels at Work," *Scandinavian Journal of Work and Organizational Psychology*, August 30, 2016, https://www.sjwop.com/articles/10.16993/sjwop.13/.

- Bring instruments to the office and have a fun musical jam session.

- Start a lunchtime book club or arts and crafts group.

- Play trivia with teammates for five minutes.

- Enjoy a fifteen-minute fitness challenge with colleagues, walking flights of stairs together or doing wall sits or planks around the office.

- Enjoy a five-minute dance break with your team.

- Have a cup of tea or coffee with someone.

- Set up a community puzzle that teammates can work on for a few minutes at a time.

- Have impromptu push-ups or sit-ups competitions.

- Throw a ball or frisbee with someone.

- Spend five or ten minutes with your team answering a fun question of the day.

The ideas for easy play breaks are endless. For a more exhaustive list of ideas, go to kristiherold.com/resources, and if you have fun ideas to share, please email me at kristi@jamgroup.

com, so we can highlight your organization and ideas in our blog and social media posts.

As company and team leaders, you can encourage your team members to take energy-boosting breaks. You can also provide ideas as well as props, tools, and resources to help make it happen. With frequent short breaks throughout the workday, your employees will enjoy energy boosts, and you will benefit from a higher level of productivity from your people.

Chapter 4 Key Takeaway Points

→ As play releases endorphins in our bodies, it naturally helps boost our energy and offset the effects of stress and burnout

→ Playful activities during the workday, either in the workplace or in remote or virtual settings, serve as powerful connections to unify and energize employees as teammates

→ When playing team sports and games, whether winning or losing, camaraderie develops that carries over into the workplace

→ Taking mini breaks throughout the day and week provides the energizing, restorative effects of taking a mini vacation

→ Even if it may feel counterintuitive, encouraging employees to take breaks will boost their energy and productivity

Play breaks also serve another important purpose: play inspires creativity. And increased creativity leads to innovation and improvement, which all the top companies prize.

PLAY Increases Creativity

*"If you get anything creative going, then the work
and play thing is the same thing, I feel."*

—EDDIE IZZARD

E very company wants to be seen as innovative, and with good reason. Innovation leads to all kinds of benefits, from growing into new markets to operating more efficiently.

Innovation happens faster and more easily when companies foster and reward creativity, and the good news is that it's fairly simple and inexpensive to get your employees to be more creative. One easy outlet for fostering creativity is increasing the opportunity for playtime.

Research shows that taking time to play will help to make us more creative. Stuart Brown is the founder of the National Institute for Play.[23] He has spent his career studying play and its effects on adults. Brown has also consulted on how to incorporate play into the workplace for Fortune 500 companies. "During play, the brain is making sense of itself through simulation and testing," he writes. "Play activity is actually helping sculpt the brain. In play, we can imagine and experience situations we have never encountered before and learn from them." When you think about it, this makes a lot of sense and seems quite obvious.

This is because innovations and new ideas don't come from doing the same thing over and over. They come from exploration and discovery, just as playing with LEGO did when we were children (or adults...anyone else reading this like me and guilty of buying LEGO for your child's birthday gift because *you* wanted to create it yourself?).

---

[23] "Play Isn't Kid Stuff: Play is Wellness," National Institute for Play, accessed May 12, 2022, https://www.nifplay.org/#Section_1.

"We've always done it this way" is one of the most dangerous phrases in business. Organizations can easily get set in their ways and be repetitive in how they do things. Playing together with our work teammates creates opportunities for sparks of creativity to fly—sparks that lead to the innovative ideas your company will benefit from.

Find a Better Way Award

At JAM, one of our core values is "find a better way." Because we are believers in really breathing life into our core values, and not just having them as words on a wall (although we do that too), we celebrate our team with the Find a Better Way seasonal award. In each season at our "Season Finals" all-hands meeting, we reflect on how the past few months have gone and look ahead to what we want to accomplish in the coming months. We celebrate new teammates who joined us during the past season, and we reflect on who the core value award winners had been each month during the season. Finally, we wrap up with our Find a Better Way (FABW) award.

Any of our staff—whether an intern or leadership—can nominate someone for the FABW award. People can even nominate themselves if they wish. The point is to honor someone who was responsible for an especially impactful idea or change that was instituted during the past season. Once all the nominations are gathered, our leadership narrows them down to a top ten list, and we put it to a vote among our entire team. Then, at Season Finals we announce the top three winners, each of whom receive a cash prize: $100 for third, $200 for second place, and $300 for first place. We do this because we are looking to inspire creativity and change among our team.

As Einstein so brilliantly said, "Insanity is doing the same thing over and over again expecting different results." If we want our organization to keep growing as leaders in our industry, we must always be looking for ways to improve. Our Find a Better Way award is integral to this effort in that it helps inspire our amazing team to actively embrace this mindset as well.

Laughter Releases Feel-Good Hormones That Boost Creativity

In Chapter 3, I talked about the feel-good hormones that are released when we play. In addition to providing all kinds of physical and mental health benefits by elevating our moods and reducing stress, these hormones also improve creativity.

When we play, a natural occurrence tends to be laughter, and one of the great perks of the act of laughing is that it releases those very same feel-good hormones that do each of us a world of good.

Many studies and articles have been written about the power of laughter, suggesting the following:[24]

- Laughter is a healthy way to overcome stress

- Laughter improves quality of life

- Laughter therapy has a positive effect on the immune system

- Laughter decreases stress-making hormones

- Laughter releases endorphins, which help you feel positive and energized

What's more, the simple act of laughing with others fosters a sense of camaraderie and strengthens relationships and trust.

---

[24] Lawrence Robinson, Melinda Smith, and Jeanne Segal, "Laughter Is the Best Medicine," Help Guide, July, 2021, https://www.helpguide .org/articles/mental-health/laughter-is-the-best-medicine.htm.

As it turns out, there is also a direct correlation between laughing and creativity. That's because of the feel-good hormone, dopamine, that laughter releases. According to an article in *Scientific American*, higher levels of dopamine motivate us to explore and boost our creativity levels.[25]

The article points out that dopamine makes us want things. This hormone drives us to explore not only our physical world but our ideas. Dopamine can help us better engage with creative activities and generate groundbreaking new concepts.

The connection is pretty clear. Playing with others makes you laugh. Laughter releases energizing endorphins and creativity-boosting dopamine. This great combo of feel-good hormones is fertile breeding ground for creative thinking and idea generation.

---

[25] Scott Barry Kaufman and Carolyn Gregoire, "How to Cultivate Your Creativity [Book Excerpt]," *Scientific American,* January 1, 2016, https://www.scientificamerican.com/article/how-to-cultivate-your -creativity-book-excerpt/.

We believe so strongly in the power of laughter at JAM that we offer our corporate clients a "Laughter Guarantee." When your team signs up for a JAM event, we guarantee there will be laughs or your money back!

Productivity vs. Creativity

Some people use the terms productivity and creativity interchangeably, but they really are very different concepts—and in a successful organization, you need both.

Productivity is all about how much the workforce produces in terms of goods, services, or work accomplished in a given length of time. When you have more energy, you can be more productive at work and get more done in a shorter time. Playtime boosts energy, which leads to being more productive.

Creativity, on the other hand, is more about the ability to come up with new, original ideas and possibilities that, when applied, can lead to something of value. I like to think of creativity as sparks of ideas and innovations.

When we play, we have the chance to explore and discover why or how things are done within a certain framework. Play lets us try new things and experiences, and in that process, we can find new solutions. In the workplace setting, play can and does lead to unexpected discoveries and solutions to the types of problems organizations everywhere face as they strive to remain relevant and innovative in a constantly changing business landscape.

The Power of Random Collisions

There is a certain measure of unpredictability to creativity. Sometimes, creative sparks can fly seemingly at random. We don't know in advance what types of creative ideas will materialize, when they'll pop up, or where they will take us, but we do know that the journey will be exciting and worth it, and sometimes very fruitful.

Which brings up something that Bruce Poon Tip, founder of G Adventures, pointed out to me. He said that when people connect and play outside of work, random collisions happen. People who otherwise might not meet or work together in the office end up having beautiful connections when provided the opportunity to play together. And from these random collisions and interactions, all sorts of great things can happen, including these:

- Bonds develop and strengthen

- New ideas and innovations form

- Post-playtime collaborations become more powerful

- More creativity comes into the organization

So much innovation can emerge from the social bonds that form and the exchange of ideas that happens when playtime leads to random interactions. When you add trust to the mix, the results can be even more powerful, as we'll see in the following story.

Bud Brainstorms, aka Blue Sky Sessions

We always try to host an annual all-hands meeting with our full-time team that is at least two to three days long. Sometimes these sessions are hosted locally, or a short bus ride from Toronto. And if we hit a big goal we've set for ourselves, we will take our full team to a sunny resort destination. These events always have meetings, planned work sessions, and playful team-bonding events scheduled into them. While the meeting topics vary from year to year, one thing we always include is what many would call blue sky sessions. We've always affectionately referred to them as our "Bud Brainstorms" (note: "Bud" was short for Budweiser, not a plant).

We book the session for an hour and a half before dinner, everyone grabs a beverage of choice—many grabbing a Budweiser or beer of some sort—and we get started with some playful icebreaker games to get everyone loosened up and laughing. Then we ask one or two questions of the group. We always make it clear there is *no wrong answer*. No one is allowed to shut down any idea. *All ideas* get written down. We encourage everyone on our team to share at least one idea. Many share multiple ideas, which is highly encouraged. Volume is good. You never know what beautiful fires will be created from all the little sparks being tossed out by different people.

Once we pull all the ideas out in a big group session, we then distill them down to our favorites and break into smaller groups, so that we can hash out the pros and cons of the top ideas—and keep fleshing them out further and further, until we have realistic changes and improvements we can envision getting made in our organization.

We have had a number of great, creative, new initiatives that were born from these playful sessions. One idea was for a new offering of our "All Sorts of Sports" league. Another year, it was during one of these Bud Brainstorms that we came up with the "keep playing" tagline for our organization.

It is from playful sessions like these that creativity abounds. And this is how we as a team continue to find a better way and make changes that will positively improve our organization and our service for our customers.

With Greater Trust, Ideas Are Shared More Freely

When we play together, we become more vulnerable with one another. From this, a level of trust begins to develop.

And when we talk with someone we trust, we feel more confident sharing our ideas, even our most out-there concepts.

Say you're in a meeting. The person running it has set up an agenda that, due to time constraints, is strictly adhered to. Do you think innovative ideas will come from this? Probably not. In a structured meeting, there is little to no room for exploration, discovery, new ideas, or innovations.

But when different members of your organization are playing together, building camaraderie, rapport, and trust, they start to get comfortable with one another. In these informal settings, creativity can begin to really flow. People feel more at ease, which means they're not as restricted about what to say or not to say.

Playtime creates a more free-flowing, anything-goes energy that allows for a freer exchange of ideas. Some of these ideas may not go anywhere, but others might be true gems that become the seeds of great innovation. When you play together, you build a level of trust that lets you share more freely, and from this sharing, great concepts can materialize.

When My Team PLAYs Together

At JAM, when our team plays together, we come up with new ideas for our business all the time. If we create a new game that everyone gets excited by, we then try to brainstorm how to package and sell it to our clients, so they can have fun with it too. Our own playtime has generated ideas for awesome products that we later sell to other companies.

A while back we had a silly games night at our office. One teammate created a particular challenge that involved two people racing each other using office chairs. We grabbed floor hockey sticks from our storage cupboard, and the race was on! Racers had to propel themselves from one end of the office to the other while sitting in office chairs, using hockey sticks to push themselves and maneuver. Another game involved having to eat donuts off a string hanging above us, with our hands behind our backs.

JAM—Office Olympics

The event was completely ridiculous, but everyone was into it. People were laughing and cheering. Everyone's energy levels went way up. We were having a blast.

And from this impromptu, random game that a teammate created, we came to realize that we had the makings of a great idea: we could go into anyone's corporate offices and create fun games for people to play using whatever they happened to already have at their location.

This innovation allows us to plan a fun office event for clients without having to book a venue, perfect for anyone on a tighter budget. The idea is that we're so good at getting people playing and laughing that we can create fun and engaging games on the spot. It's a new angle on what we already provide to our clients, and with a little more development, we'll be bringing this innovation to fruition. For a top five list and videos of playful, quick games you can set up for your team in your office, go to kristiherold.com/resources.

Our Surprise and Delight Initiative

At JAM we run a book club. We read everything from biographies to business books and more. When we read books together, which to me is another form of play, talking about what we learn from them is a great way to spark creative ideas.

In fact, we've implemented a number of new initiatives that have come from our time playing together through reading books and sharing what each of us discovers. After reading a great book called *The Customer Service Revolution* by John DiJulius, our team was inspired to start our own "Surprise and Delight" initiative in order to really wow our clients and hopefully help us to create *Raving Fans* (yet another book we have read as part of our office book club, by Ken Blanchard and Sheldon M. Bowles).

For the Surprise and Delight initiative, everyone from our customer service team was given a small budget to spend money for the purpose of surprising and delighting our customers. As an example, one of my teammates from customer service had to let a sports team in our leagues know that their opponents were unable to get enough people together and they were going to be defaulting their game (never news we enjoy having to share). Our staff suggested they could still go use the softball diamond to practice, but the response was that this team would instead have a fun team BBQ together at their captain's house. Our service team decided this would be a great opportunity to surprise and delight, so they had one of our ELFs (Evening League Facilitator) drop off a case of beer for the team's impromptu BBQ.

As it turned out, this became a huge double win. Not only did the softball team absolutely love what we did for them and become raving fans, but a few days later we heard from the brand manager at the beer company who was our current league sponsor. They had coincidentally been on the team that had a case of our sponsor's beer dropped off—and were thrilled to see our Surprise and Delight program in action, especially because we were taking the opportunity to highlight our sponsor's product as well! Overall, what was a negative situation became a positive, our clients loved it, and this all happened because our team was inspired and engaged to surprise and delight our customers in a playful way.

Had we not taken the time for those fun literary interactions and creative discussions as a team, ideas and initiatives like Surprise and Delight would not have come to fruition.

PLAY Doesn't Have an Agenda

Any business that makes the time to play and laugh together is not wasting its time or resources. On the contrary, play should not be looked at as an expense but rather as an investment in innovating and finding better ways to operate. When people get together to play, in whatever way works for them, that's where sparks of creativity happen that lead to innovative ideas and initiatives.

Play is about having no agenda and seeing what beautiful surprises pop up. In a work meeting with an agenda that everyone's following, participants tend to simply plow through the list, point by point. When it's over, everyone goes back to their desks and resumes their jobs. There's not much room for new initiatives there.

But during play, which is largely unstructured and agenda-free, people are connecting and having fun together. What comes from that is always a surprise, and it often can lead to innovations.

PLAY Breaks Down Hierarchy and Evens the Playing Field

Sometimes in meetings, certain teammates feel intimidated to speak up or offer their opinions. Have you yourself ever experienced this fear, or perhaps witnessed a coworker in this situation?

This is pretty common in the workplace, particularly with more junior employees, those new to an organization, or anyone who feels outranked by others in attendance. Someone may have a great idea that can be a complete game-changer for the company, but it's never heard because the person holds back, unwilling to speak up or perhaps fearful of rocking the boat.

Play helps to remove those barriers. It breaks down hierarchy and places everyone on a more equal playing field. When we have book club sessions, for example, everyone is encouraged to contribute. Everyone gets the same length of floor time to talk about their perspectives on a book we all read. And it doesn't matter if the person sharing ideas is the CEO or the most junior person on the team; play encourages everyone to participate equally.

Whether you're playing a soccer game, playing in a band, or playing a virtual escape room with your work team, it makes no difference who is the company president, who is a customer service rep, an accountant, a junior marketer, a cafeteria worker, or a developer. Everyone is in it together. Everyone's having fun and contributing, working together to try to win as a team. With a more even playing field and the removal of corporate hierarchy, playtime lets anyone speak up without feeling intimidated.

PLAY Opens Opportunities to Share Ideas and Build Trust

When a bunch of people from an organization get together to play and ignore corporate hierarchy, their guard goes down. They're no longer on the defensive. As a result, people feel a higher level of trust, boosting their confidence to speak up and be themselves. With a playful mindset, people are willing to try or say new things when, otherwise, they might feel too self-conscious.

That new junior marketing person just might feel emboldened to share great ideas with their teammates while playing that they wouldn't dare share with senior-level marketing people in a formal meeting. When everyone's playing volleyball or doing a scavenger hunt together, and the hierarchy boundaries start to dissolve, the junior marketer's innovative ideas have a greater chance to surface and be heard. Barriers are broken, enabling creative sparks to happen at all levels.

Once these bonds of friendship and personal connection have started to form in a playful environment, it becomes much easier for work teammates to feel they can trust the people on their team. When we have trust, we are more apt to allow ourselves to be vulnerable in work meetings. When we feel safe among our team—whom we've gotten to know better through play—we are more open to sharing ideas at work that we may otherwise have sat on. We are also more prone to ask questions in order to get clarity and more ready to be honest and candid with feedback. All of this benefits the organization, and it is all a result of the healthier, more trusting relationships that have developed through play.

The Need to Be Creative

Humans love to be creative. They need it. Crave it. In the workplace, nourishing that creative spark is essential.

None of us are built to just stuff ourselves into suits or other work clothes and type on our computer keyboards creating spreadsheets and PowerPoint presentations all day long. We need to mix it up with playful experiences to boost the type of creativity that leads to innovation.

Employees benefit. Leaders benefit. Entire organizations benefit from playtime. It's an essential part of doing business.

Top Companies Value Creativity and PLAYtime

I recently read the Boston Consulting Group's (BCG) innovative companies report,[26] which lists the top fifty most innovative companies annually. The report has found that in the years following the financial crisis of 2008–2009, the publicly traded members of Boston Consulting Group's 2007 ranking of the 50 Most Innovative Companies outperformed the broader market on shareholder return by 5.6 percent a year through the end of 2019. Further, the data suggests that successful self-disruptors earned an annual premium in shareholder return of 2.7 percentage points from 2016 to 2019 over companies that focused solely on defending their own turf. The report notes that the innovators that outperform

---

[26] "Serial Innovators Outperform in Times of Recovery," Boston Consulting Group, June 22, 2020, https://www.bcg.com/press/22june2020-most -innovative-companies-2020-the-serial-innovation-imperative.

their big-company peers also put more money behind their innovation programs—1.4 times more as a percentage of sales—and they get far greater payoffs: four times as much as a percentage of sales. These leaders recognize that investing in innovation is fundamental to their growth and success and that doing so will provide significant returns.

SPENDING ON INNOVATION

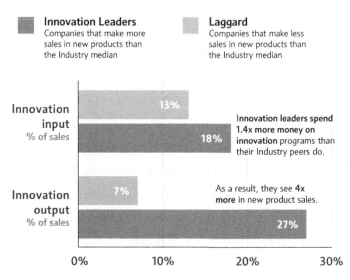

Data Includes companies with sales >$18.
Source: Boston Consulting Group, "The Most Innovative Companies 2020."

It was reaffirming to see that seven of the top ten 2020 most innovative companies (Apple, Amazon, Microsoft, Samsung,

Huawei, IBM, and Facebook)[27] are all *repeat* clients of JAM. Clearly, these innovative organizations invest in play for their teams as well.

Organizations that have made it big worldwide certainly value the creative sparks that lead to innovation. Take a look at two household names, Microsoft and Google.

At Microsoft, PLAY Isn't Just a Perk

For this multinational tech giant, playing is a big part of the company's culture. Microsoft hosts their OpenHack events: developer-focused engagements that connect open development teams with experts to tackle a series of real-world challenges through hands-on, fun experimentation online. These events provide a breeding ground for innovation while playing and working in a tech setting.

The company puts a lot of focus on the employee experience and stresses innovation, creativity, and collaboration. With the goal of engaging and empowering their employees,

---

[27]   Carmen Ang, "Ranked: The 50 Most Innovative Companies," Visual Capitalist, July 17, 2020, https://www.visualcapitalist.com/top-50-most-innovative-companies-2020/.

Microsoft has developed a data-driven approach to building corporate culture and improving its employee experience.

Company leaders believe in building a foundation that provides stability and consistency, and upon this, creativity and collaboration are added to bring more meaningful experiences to employees. Microsoft does everything it can to support its employees, so they can be more creative and innovative in their jobs.

Microsoft participated in research that illuminated the need for play and the value people place on playing. Top findings included the following: [28]

- In the United States, 70 percent of employees feel more energized when they're allowed time to play at work

- Only 31 percent of employees in the US feel their companies facilitate playing at work

---

[28] "Reinventing Microsoft's Employee Experience for a Hybrid World," Microsoft, February 3, 2022, https://www.microsoft.com/en-us/inside track/reinventing-the-employee-experience-at-microsoft.

- Over half of employees report that their new ideas come from doing something playful or spending time with friends

Google's Push for a Happy, Productive Workforce

The search engine, advertising, and cloud computing colossus is, for many, the company to emulate with regard to creating opportunities for play at work. Google's desire to foster the happiest and most productive work environment is behind this push for more playtime.

Google offices are great at creating playful vibes. These are just some of the tools of the trade for Google locations around the world:

- LEGO brick play stations

- Scavenger hunts

- Walls to scribble on

- Office putting greens

- Tube slides

- Rooftop decks

- Bikes and scooters for indoor use

- Bowling alleys

- Climbing walls

- Beach volleyball

- TGIF celebrations

- Workspace hammocks

- Secret reading rooms

- Yoga classes

The company strives to make work fun—not just to get employees to show up but to encourage playful interactions. This fosters friendships, which in turn strengthens loyalty. It also gets employees' creative juices flowing, so they can be more innovative in everything they do.

Creative People Solve Problems More Easily

Why do companies want to innovate? Because innovation solves problems. It brings organizations a competitive edge. Being innovative means thinking outside of the box. Since play cultivates creativity, it is key to helping organizations be more innovative in all areas.

Strong business leaders are always looking to find better ways to do things. This requires an openness to change, being creative and innovative, and not getting stuck in a rut.

Creative people are able to solve problems faster and come up with better solutions because they're not set in their ways. They get excited by new ideas and seeing creative sparks fly.

One obvious choice that you, as a leader, can make in order to encourage creativity among your team is to establish time for your employees to play. Build play into your budget and schedule. As your business grows and you seek the best ways to do things, continuously look for opportunities to boost and bring out your team's creativity. Doing so will help build creativity among all your employees, so that everyone can learn how to solve problems more easily and get those innovative sparks flying. The benefits of creative innovation will be felt internally among your staff and externally by your customers and will also affect your bottom line.

Chapter 5 Key Takeaway Points

→ Organizations can innovate more easily when they encourage and reward creativity

→ Playful activities that lead to plenty of laughter and social interactions release feel-good hormones, like dopamine and endorphins, that help people become more creative and come up with groundbreaking concepts

→ Play develops greater trust between teammates, breaking barriers by eliminating hierarchies and allowing for people at all levels to share their innovative ideas more openly

→ Companies known as some of the most innovative in the world value creativity and develop ongoing opportunities for their employees to play

→ When people are more creative, they come up with better solutions

Creative employees are more empowered and engaged, typically feel happier, and thus serve clients better, too, leading to higher levels of customer satisfaction.

PLAY Creates Happier Customers

"People are at their most mindful when they are at play. If we find ways of enjoying our work, blurring the lines between work and play, the gains will be greater."

—ELLEN LANGER

According to a Gallup report,[29] happy and engaged employees are more likely to improve customer relationships, resulting in a 20 percent increase in sales.

---

[29] Shep Hyken, "How Happy Employees Make Happy Customers," *Forbes*, May 27, 2017, https://www.forbes.com/sites/shephyken/2017/05/27/how-happy-employees-make-happy-customers/?sh=32aad01a5c35.

Barry Glassman (whom I introduced you to in Chapter 1) also believes that a playful culture like the one they have at Glassman Wealth directly benefits clients. Which means *everyone* benefits—employees, customers, and the organization's bottom line. We have all experienced talking on the phone with an employee of a company, and we can tell almost immediately if that employee is happy or unhappy in their work. Even on the phone, their level of happiness and job satisfaction comes across in their voice and how they serve us. As customers, we notice this and will make decisions and judgments about an organization based on our interactions with their employees. In some cases, we may decide we don't like the organization anymore and don't want to continue dealing with them.

Clients appreciate interacting with upbeat employees—they tend to be attentive and deliver a higher quality of service. When interactions with your staff are positive, customer satisfaction increases, which can improve client retention and business profitability.

Most business leaders would agree that a key to a company's success is an ongoing stream of happy customers willing to pay for the company's goods and services. And then retaining them—getting them to come back—again and again, year after year. Retaining loyal customers is far less expensive than finding new ones, so it makes sense that happy employees = happy customers = happy profits.

A meta-analysis done by the London School of Economics (LSE), assessing almost 2 million employees across over 82,000 different business units, found that there is a positive correlation between employee happiness and customer loyalty, productivity, and profitability, and not surprisingly a negative correlation between their happiness and turnover. Simply put, the happier your employees are, the more profitable your organization will be for a variety of reasons.

EMPLOYEE SATISFACTION AND FIRM PERFORMANCE

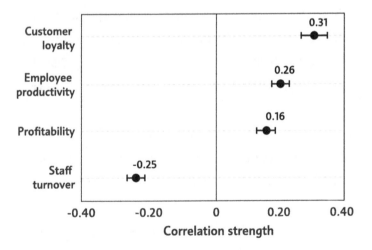

Throughout this book, we've explored and shown how play increases employees' energy levels, leading to more productivity, and how it also boosts physical and mental well-being. It stands to reason that when we as employers create time for our teams to play, their boosts in energy and happiness will improve interactions with our customers, who will now enjoy a much richer, more rewarding experience.

When an employee's positive attitude spills over into consumer relationships, the ripple effects are many, as this next example from Deloitte demonstrates.

From a Partner at Deloitte

One of the Big Four accounting and professional services networks, Deloitte, provides audit, taxation, corporate finances, and legal services to Fortune 500 companies and other organizations globally. Deloitte is on both the US and Canadian lists of LinkedIn's top 50 companies to grow your career.

I've had the pleasure of connecting with Marissa Lewis, a partner at Deloitte, on multiple occasions, since Deloitte is a JAM client, and she shared this account with me.

Marissa was initially introduced to JAM events via one of

her clients, for whom she was working as the lead on a project. The client invited Marissa and her team to join them for a playful JAM event, and she and her colleagues agreed to attend.

The evening of the event, Marissa wasn't sure she was up for it. She'd had a really long day. She was tired and feeling a bit grumpy. On top of that, she had a headache and wasn't in the mood for a virtual social event. Nevertheless, she joined in because, having been invited by her client, she felt obligated to do so.

She was not expecting all the benefits that came her way from participating in that event. First, there were immediate results for her own personal well-being. Later on, she saw additional benefits in the form of improved relationships between her team and their client.

A Totally Different Level of Engagement

Immersed in the virtual event, Marissa found herself having a great time. She ended up laughing for the entire hour.

Interacting with the client in a playful activity created a stronger bond between her team and their client, which took their professional relationship to a whole new level of engagement. After the event, many positive emails flowed between both sides, increasing the happiness factor for both the Deloitte team and their client.

"After playing together," Marissa noted, "our team felt more joyful and bonded. Taking that little bit of time to play definitely helped strengthen our cross-team collaboration, which inevitably led to better work for our clients."

Everyone benefited. Stronger bonds formed, and everyone experienced an exchange of great energy that came from the camaraderie and goodwill that developed during this play-time. Marissa feels her team was able to deliver even more exceptional service because they'd engaged with the client at a fun and more personal level. That experience inspired her to book more playful events for her own team internally.

That positive boost of energy that Marissa's team feels every time they take the opportunity to play continues to ripple out to all the clients they serve. The employees are a happier bunch, and this continues to extend out in the form of a higher level of service to Deloitte's clients.

Judging by the positive emails Marissa receives from happy

clients, the time that her team takes to play is paying off beautifully in creating cross-team collaborations and delivering higher-quality service to their clients.

Combating the Loneliness of Working from Home

Another benefit of playing together virtually that Marissa has noticed is that it combats the loneliness many remote workers feel working from home. The hours are long, coworkers aren't around, and while there are great benefits from being able to work remotely, it can also be very challenging for mental health. Opportunities to play alleviate this loneliness.

A *Harvard Business Review* article I read recently talked about organizations it had researched that were reporting high levels of exhaustion among employees. Interestingly, it was discovered through their research that it wasn't the pace of work that had these employees feeling exhausted. Rather, it was because people were feeling lonely. When we are lonely, we get lethargic, and this is something that employers can help to change. By providing opportunities for our teams to engage with each other through play, we are providing the much-needed opportunity for human connection.

As Marissa from Deloitte expressed, "Having made time for some playful interactions has us working happier as a team, and as a team, we're willing to go over and above for each other. And our productivity is so much better."

PLAY Has a Powerful
Ripple Effect

Happiness is contagious. When people play together, they not only experience happiness, but they spread it. After a round of frisbee golf or a softball game or a musical theater rehearsal, people go home happier. They're happier parents, happier significant others, happier roommates. They spread joy within their own circles.

And when they wake up the next day, they're a little happier going into the workplace or their Zoom calls because they had fun playing the day before. So they are happier coworkers or team leaders, and the joy continues to spread.

From one person playing a sport or engaging in a group activity and having fun, sharing a laugh with others, a ripple effect happens. That happiness spreads. People who make time for play in their lives are happier within themselves and thus nicer to and more willing to help out their colleagues.

They will inevitably be friendlier with their customers as well, providing overall better service.

Taking time to play makes everyone happier, creating a ripple effect that emanates out to others, including families, friends, coworkers, and clients.

Happier Teams Create Sunnier Interactions

When people are happier in the workplace, they deliver better service.

What makes people happier? There are a lot of things that go into ensuring our people are happy at work, but one very easy one is having laughs together. As mentioned earlier, the endorphins released in our bodies when we have a laugh promote an overall sense of well-being. As a manager, when you encourage your team to make time for some laughs, you foster a happier group of employees who will be happier providing service to your customers as well.

With customer-facing roles, you better believe the customer at the other end of the phone or video call can tell whether or not an employee is happy in their job. We've all been customers ourselves, and we all know what it's like when speaking with someone who is not a happy camper. Not a good time for anyone involved. On the flip side, we all know what a positive and fun experience it can be when we are talking to someone who is clearly very happy and engaged with their job.

My friend Tracey Ivanyshyn is the former CEO of UPLevel, a contact care center with over 120 employees. She describes the organization's purpose as "curating exceptional conversations and highly effective connections that deliver results for their clients." UPLevel has been recognized on Canada's Top 100 Employers list as well as nominated multiple times for Canada's 10 Most Admired Corporate Cultures. In conjunction with this recognition for their incredible culture, UPLevel has also been on the Profit 200 List of Canada's Fastest-Growing Companies. These amazing results show that a strong culture and profit growth can (and do) go hand in hand.

UPLevel has had a passion for culture for a very long time— far before it was cool. Turnover among staff in the contact center world is usually quite high with the industry average sitting at less than two years. At UPLevel, their average head office employee tenure is over nine years, about 350 percent better than their industry average. The leadership team at

UPLevel believes in investing in a fun workplace culture because they know that happy employees who feel appreciated and empowered will help to build a great organization. The passion for culture at UPLevel has added value to the lives of their employees, their customers, and the bottom line of the company.

At UPLevel, play and fun is intentional, not an afterthought. Inside the organization, they have developed a "village" structure such that every person is part of a village responsible for customized culture creation, with a mayor, a tourism board, a welcoming committee, and more. And they regularly host events like coffee house talent shows, dance parties, and parking lot parties.

Early in the pandemic, UPLevel turned to JAM for help creating memorable time for play within their team. Their staff gave such rave reviews of their experiences connecting and laughing that they decided they wanted to extend these opportunities for play to their clients.

Similar to Inertia Design, the UPLevel team was looking for original gift ideas for their clients, and instead of giving a branded gift that no one really wants, they decided to celebrate their relationships with their clients by giving them the gift of playful experiences. They held events creating mixed teams combining their employees with their clients, ensuring folks at all levels could get to know one another—and the camaraderie and connections that were created have been phenomenal. One client enjoyed the experience so much that they've since requested two "rematches," and the ongoing trash talk continues in a fun-filled way, reminding everyone of the great bonds they've developed. As Tracey said, "It is so much fun seeing people open up and let those playful parts of themselves shine. These are real connections, and they are priceless."

Not Just for Customer-Facing Roles

I want to emphasize that the benefits to customers that come from employees who are happier thanks to opportunities for play aren't tied just to customer-facing roles. Every employee matters and has a responsibility to the organization's end customer—whether developers writing code for clients they'll never meet, designers creating beautiful ad designs, accountants balancing the books, researchers developing new meds, or anyone who never sees or talks to customers directly. These non-customer-facing employees will also benefit from a boost in happiness when provided with playtime opportunities.

Consider this: nobody ever wants to upset a restaurant server because we know that when they're out of sight, they could do something rather untoward to our food if we're acting like jerks and treating them poorly. But it's more than that too. Just think: how successful have you ever been at getting a charge reversed when you lose your temper with an employee over the phone?

If your clients are relying on the next great software product or update from your company, but your developers are overworked, stressed out, and short-tempered because of too much pressure to perform and not enough outlets to play, you might experience significant delays in that product or patch getting done. Or it might get done by the deadline but be riddled with errors, creating dissatisfied clients who may flock to Google to give one-star reviews and badmouth your organization at every turn.

Extrapolating from these examples, we can say that whether employees are unhappy due to internal stresses from their work team or external stresses from miserable customers or other issues, unhappy employees are unlikely to give customers the best service they are capable of. They may even do things to deliver subpar work if they're upset and disenchanted enough.

Unhappy employees can damage your organization in ways we may not even realize, while happy, energized employees are typically more motivated to give their best, whatever their job may be.

Treat your employees right, provide opportunities for them to play and be happier at work, and they'll do right by you and your customers and company. Play (or the lack of) affects everyone.

"How Happy Are You" Metrics

Tricia Carroll is the head of people operations at Acceleration Partners (AP), a marketing organization that employs 250 people full-time. AP was a remote-first organization (well before the pandemic ever started the remote-work trend) that was founded by my friend and incredibly wise entrepreneur, Robert Glazer. AP actively strives to include a lot of playful initiatives to help keep everyone on their team, especially as they are majority remote workers, connected, engaged, and motivated.

For example, on Slack they have a "What made your week?" channel that lets people share their highlights from work and personal experiences during the week. They have also mastered the art of having fun virtually, hosting everything from happy hours to costume parties online.

Tricia emphasizes that AP recognizes that employees can't focus just on work. One of their monthly key performance indicators (KPIs) revolves around asking all employees this question: how happy are you at work on a scale of one to five?

AP strives to maintain a score of four and above for everyone. The company has found that, by focusing on that as a metric, it's paid off in a lot of ways. It's helped them with everything from customer retention to company growth.

Known For Amazing Customer Service

The online shoe and clothing retailer Zappos is known for outstanding customer service. They've figured out that happier employees lead to happier customers. Since moving into new company headquarters in Las Vegas in 2013, Zappos has focused on reimagining their office spaces for both work and play.

The company provides an abundance of indoor and outdoor spaces where employees can meet for impromptu chats to connect with each other. In addition, Zappos has a jam room full of musical instruments, as well as game rooms with Ping-Pong tables and other recreational equipment. They also have an outdoor nine-hole mini putt golf course on site.

The company believes that when its people are free to create and innovate, good things happen for everyone. Zappos launched in 1999 and has since grown to over $500 million in annual sales. Since 2016, Zappos has continued to see steady revenue growth every year. Zappos recognizes that employees are happier when they feel more valued. They know that when employees are happier, customers are happier, and the organization as a whole will thrive.

Customer-Focused Fun and Surprises

Since its beginnings in 1998, JetBlue (called NewAir back then) chose to take a playful, customer-centric approach to doing business. The airline operates under the philosophy that great service can come only from a positive company culture. JetBlue's leadership reasons that placing a high priority on creating a strong culture leads to team members who are happy with their jobs and share that joy with their customers.

The organization's culture is built upon respecting and trusting employees and fostering open communication. From this, great traditions have developed. One particularly fun tradition is to send JetBlue's chief people officer,[30] who has the important role of engaging crew members and championing the company culture, to airports and onto flights with the purpose of surprising customers with rewards, gifts, and playing games like in-flight trivia games, often giving away plane tickets as prizes.[31]

Right from the start of JetBlue's launching (despite the 9/11 terrorist attacks in 2001), it has seen strong expansion and growth. Since its launch over twenty years ago (with the exception of the COVID-19 pandemic), JetBlue has had consistent and impressive revenue growth, expanding to be one of the top airlines in the US.

---

[30] "JetBlue Names Laurie Villa Chief People Officer," jetBlue Blog, May 25, 2021, http://mediaroom.jetblue.com/investor-relations/press-releases /2021/05-25-2021-150015329.

[31] "Chief People Officer is a Real People Person," jetBlue Blog, 2020, http://blog.jetblue.com/chief-people-officer-is-a-real-people-person/.

JetBlue's operating revenue from FY 2011 to FY 2020 (in million US dollars)

OPERATING REVENUE ($ MILLIONS)

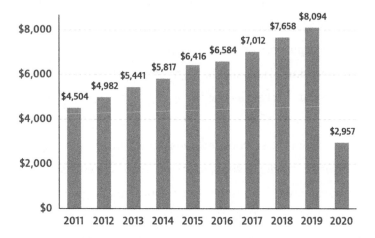

Building a fantastic culture internally and ensuring a happier team of employees has definitely been one of JetBlue's keys to exceptional customer service for the traveling public.

Working Hard and PLAYing Hard

In the right business culture, working and playing can go hand in hand. When work is more fun and rewarding, it can feel a lot like play, even with everyone working their hardest to create outstanding customer experiences.

Herb Kelleher, who was the CEO of Southwest Airlines, was asked, "How do you get all your employees to smile as you do?"

He said, "We hire smiley people."

Not only has Southwest shown steady revenue growth in the decade before the pandemic, but they are also well-renowned for their development of a fun-loving culture that values all the following:[32]

- Employee happiness

- Customers

- Humor

- Quirky on-board announcements from crew members

- Connecting people to what's important to them

- Empathy

---

[32] Gustavo Razzetti, "Mapping Southwest's Fun, Loving Culture," Fearless Culture, January 12, 2020, https://www.fearlessculture.design/blog-posts/southwest-airlines-culture-design-canvas.

- Strong personal relationships

- Valuing people's contributions

- Wowing customers

- Maintaining a fun-LUVing attitude that celebrates passion and success

This people-centered, playful approach has worked well for Southwest. Not only has the company enjoyed over forty consecutive years of profitability (pre-pandemic), but it's also number one among airlines in terms of having the lowest number of customer complaints. And an impressive 85 percent of employees indicated they're proud to work for the company.

Fun And Success Do Go Together

All these companies—Deloitte, UPLevel, Acceleration Partners, Zappos, JetBlue, Southwest—have something important in common: they put people first. They understand that people do better when they are valued and given the chance to have fun together. Successful companies like these provide real-world examples of what happens when organizations prioritize employee happiness.

These companies show that having fun and being successful are not mutually exclusive. On the contrary, having fun through play boosts employee morale, which boosts customer happiness and improves consumer relationships.

Chapter 6 Key Takeaway Points

→ Play at work and outside of work with workplace colleagues boosts employee satisfaction, which makes employees more motivated in their dealings with customers

→ Happy employees who see their jobs as fun and worthwhile will serve their clients more enthusiastically, creating superior customer experiences

→ Whether customer-facing or behind the scenes, it's just as important for employees in all roles to access happiness-boosting playtime opportunities, since end users still rely on the products or innovations being developed by these employees

→ Happier teams create sunnier interactions and stronger consumer relationships

→ Employees who play feel happier and create a happiness ripple effect around them

Companies that value people, play, and fun are some of the most successful ones around.

Just as Gallup asserts, having engaged employees leads to having happier customers. When customers love your organization, interactions will increase. Sales will go up. Profits will rise.

When you invest in your employees' happiness by creating a culture that embraces play and creates opportunities for fun social interactions, you invest in both employee and customer loyalty. From there, the sky's the limit in terms of creating and retaining customers for life.

CONCLUSION

So Why PLAY?

*"We do not stop playing because we grow old.
We grow old because we stop playing."*

—GEORGE BERNARD SHAW

Growing up in a small town in Northern Ontario with two older brothers, we were always outside playing. I was either doing my best to keep up with them and their friends (if they would let me) or organizing groups of kids in the neighborhood to play games of hide-and-seek, tag, kick the can, or my personal favorite, sardines. The rule in our house was simple: get outside and play, and be home when the streetlights turn on. Using the power of our imaginations, we would make a game out of *anything*. As we've learned throughout this book, play comes naturally to kids.

Looking back, I am extraordinarily grateful to see that play has remained a constant throughout my life. I went from organizing neighborhood kids playing outside to starting the social committee at my high school, organizing scavenger hunts and "Who dunnit?"–type games. After university I started the SSC, getting adults playing recreational sports, and then a decade or so later, I helped to start an adult community musical theater troupe. Most recently, I led the launch of our virtual and in-person corporate events business JAM, helping to connect corporate teams through play all over the world. In hindsight, I recognize that building communities and connecting people through play seems to be my passion and purpose in life.

Now, I am more excited than ever to spread the message about the power of play and its vital role in helping businesses and workplace cultures to thrive. As I've said throughout this book, the positive benefits that come when business leaders make time for play in their organizations are undeniable.

By intentionally focusing a little time and effort on fostering play at work, you and your organization will see amazing boosts in the following:

- Employee retention and loyalty

- Engagement and morale

- Physical and mental health

- Energy and productivity

- Creativity and innovation

- Customer satisfaction and retention

And last but not least, your company's bottom line!

This is important: investing in play truly impacts your P&L—it really does *pay to play*. It's not an exaggeration to say that play can transform your entire business and is just as integral to its financial health as other areas such as hiring and marketing.

In order to leverage the immense power of play, you will have to heed the call. You will want to look at your retention and eNPS scores and truly ask yourself the tough question as to whether or not your employees are really happy. And from there, you will want to start taking seriously the fundamental human need and desire for play.

Trust me: you will never regret making time and space for play in the workplace.

APPENDIX

Ideas for PLAY at Work

"Work consists of whatever a body is obliged to do.
Play consists of whatever a body
is not obliged to do."

—MARK TWAIN

Legend:

V—Virtual option

H—Hybrid option

IP—In-person option

$—low or no cost, $$—moderate cost, $$$—higher cost

Group Physical Activity

- **Walking or running groups** (V / H / IP—$)

  Organize a walking or running group for early mornings, over lunch hour, or at the end of the workday for a couple days a week. Post your planned routes and distances in advance, so everyone knows where to meet and when. Whether you are all working from an office or from home, you can still meet in person to enjoy this exercise together. Encourage people to dress for the weather. As they say in Norway, "There is no such thing as bad weather, only bad clothing."

- **Social sports teams** (V / H / IP—$$)

  Competitive or beginner, multi-sport or one focus, all options exist in every North American city. Sign up a team for an adult recreational sports league in whatever city (or cities) your staff is working in and cover the cost for them. Playing a team sport can provide an in-person connection for your staff to play together, even if you've got a remote or hybrid workforce. Consider providing company-branded team jerseys (for an extra marketing boost).

- **Sport skills clinics** (V / H / IP—$$)

  Book a one-day corporate event, and get your work team learning a new sport together—perhaps Ultimate Frisbee, beach volleyball, or curling. Have an event provider like JAM or your local adult recreational sports league line you up with coaches and field or gym or ice space for your work team to learn a new skill while being physically active together.

- *Health challenges* (V/H/IP—$)

  Create teams among your staff and have a monthly health challenge. Make a shared spreadsheet with points for different types of physical activity: planks, sit-ups, push-ups, burpees, squats, lunges, walking, running, cycling, etc. Using the honor system, encourage your staff to track the points they earn based on their activity each day. Have a small reward for the individuals and teams who earn the most points over the course of the month.

- *Recess* (IP—$)

  Bring back the best part of your schoolyard days with a midafternoon recess. Encourage your staff to get up from their desks and head outside for twenty minutes. Walk together to the nearest parking lot or green space and throw a ball or play some frisbee golf. Then head back to your desks with everyone feeling more refreshed and energized.

- *Train for an event together* (V/H/IP—$$)

  Pick an event to sign up for and train together, perhaps raising money for a charity in the process. Consider a 5K or 10K charity run, a team obstacle course, or a dragon boat race. Get volunteers from your staff who want to be part of the team, and book the event a couple months in advance. Create a training program to follow as a team, such that you can meet a couple times a week for fun training sessions together or train individually if you are living in different cities. Meeting all together in one location for the big event is a great way to see each other in person and feel the bonding over working together toward a group goal.

- **Group yoga** (V / H / IP—$)

   Hire a teacher to come into the office once a week to lead a thirty- to forty-five-minute, midmorning yoga class. Have mats in the office, and use the board room or lunchroom to get a bit of movement flowing together as a team. People working from home can be encouraged to join over Zoom.

Get Creative

- **Share Spotify lists** (V / H / IP—$)

   Once a month, pick a theme or genre of music and ask everyone to share their favorite song related to it. Then create a Spotify playlist, and send the link to everyone.

- **Have a guitar or keyboard at the office** (H / IP—$$)

   Keep a guitar and/or keyboard in the office in a central spot, like the lunchroom, so if someone wants a quick break to play some music, they can do so. You may find others gathering around to listen in or sing along.

- **Do an improv class** (V/IP—$$)

Whether virtual or in-person, hire an experienced improv coach to guide your team through a variety of improv games. There are few rules when it comes to Improv, except these guidelines:

1) Say YES

2) Say YES, and…

3) There are no mistakes

Improv brings us back to child-like curiosity and imagination and allows for fantastic blue-sky situations to be created—with lots of laughter and no judgment.

- **Plan weekly musical "jam" sessions** (H/IP—$)

Have a weekly "jam" session booked into the calendar, and invite anyone who wants to participate to bring their instrument of choice into the office on that day. Get some jamming happening over lunch or near the end of the day. This will have you connecting with your team and playing in a whole new way.

- **Rehearse for a quarterly concert** (H/IP—$)

  If you've got a group that meets regularly to "jam," consider planning a quarterly concert. Arrange to have drinks and snacks brought in after work, so you can throw a bit of a party while listening to your talented team of musicians perform. Having a performance booked will give the musicians a fun goal to work toward as they play and will also provide everyone else who doesn't play an instrument an opportunity to be supportive as audience members and part of the fun.

- **Book an after-work karaoke night for your team** (H/IP—$$)

  Head out to a local karaoke bar for after-work drinks and laughs. Perhaps the company can pick up the tab for the first round of drinks. Singing together is sure to get the laughs happening and the friendship bonds strengthening.

Team-Bonding Games

- **Virtual events** (V / H—$$)

  Book a monthly Lunch 'n' Laugh in the calendar with your team. Include the Zoom link and either plan your own fun virtual/hybrid game or hire a turnkey service provider like JAM to host an hour of laughs for your team. Play games like bingo, trivia, scavenger hunts, escape rooms, Family

Feud, and more, while connecting through laughter with your teammates in all different parts of the world—with no flight or hotel required. Keep in mind that games and events like this can be played in a hybrid-style, where some people play from the office and others from home.

- *Escape rooms* (V / H / IP—$)

  Get your team together in person, or try a virtual escape room. We've done both in-person and virtual escape rooms with our own team, as well as hosting thousands of virtual escape rooms for other corporate teams. We've also created escape room challenges that we can bring on-site to corporate offices. I love escape rooms in any format because they get teams working and playing together, creatively solving clues and challenges. It is a fun opportunity to observe how interestingly and differently each of your various teammates' minds work.

- *Office Olympics* (V / H—$$)

  We originally created this event for Adam Franklin and his team of over one hundred people at Franklin Sports, and it has become quite a popular option for many of our JAM corporate clients. Break your staff into teams, and meet for a monthly virtual/hybrid event with a little friendly competition. Keep track of the standings on an event-by-event basis, with prizes for the winning teams, and also keep a leaderboard of standings over the course of a year, with a grand prize for the winning team. Provide bonus points to teams for attendance or costumes. After each monthly event, consider allowing the losing team the opportunity to "steal" or "trade" a player from another team to keep things exciting and fresh. Such a great way to get fun competitive juices flowing on a regular basis while enjoying some laughter together.

- ***Field days*** (IP—$$$)

    Hire an outfit like JAM to run a field day event. Gather your people in one city so they can play together in person. Ensure everyone is broken into teams, with people from different departments spread across teams—so everyone can meet and connect with new faces. You can even have team shirts done up in different colors and with the company logo on them. Field day events can consist of silly games like corn-hole, Jenga, obstacle courses, shoe-toss, three-legged races, wheelbarrow races, and more. Playing games like this, where not a lot of skill is involved, can truly even the playing field and keep your team active and laughing. Organizations like JAM are experienced and innovative when it comes to making play happen; you can have them bring the fun right to your office. Event organizers typically have on hand all the games they need, and using their imagination and experience, can create fun and play opportunities anywhere, out of anything, just like we did when we were kids.

- *Mini-Olympics* (IP—$$$)

  Similar to Field Day–style events, if you want a fun in-person active gathering, a popular option to consider is a mini Olympic-style event where your teams go through a series of different sports over the course of the day, like soccer, Ultimate Frisbee, and beach or grass volleyball. Split your group into multiple teams, all with their own special team shirts. Teams earn points based on results of each game and compete toward a fun overall title.

- *Scavenger hunts/Amazing Races* (IP—$$)

  Scavenger hunts or Amazing Race–type challenges can always be organized in-house; however, you may be better off outsourcing this work to a company who does this day in and day out, so you don't have a DIY disaster on your hands. Sometimes it is better to spend a little more money upfront, so you don't have your own staff wasting time planning an event when they don't have that much experience doing so. Further, their time is likely better spent on their actual jobs. Note that scavenger hunts can be done as entirely virtual events—but you can also do them in-person for a totally different feel. Effectively, you'll want to put your group into teams, and then give them a series of things to find or challenges to accomplish. This can be done around their house if virtually, or around the office or city if in-person. Events like this can entail taking public transit, which makes for a lot of fun and adventure. And if everyone is wearing a team shirt with your company logo on it, you're getting some fun marketing at the same time, as people in the streets will be sure to notice groups of adults running around doing silly poses and laughing together as they search for clues around the city. Teams are given time limits and meeting points for spot checks, and finish when points are tallied to come up with a winning team.

Get To Know Each Other

- ***Eat lunch together*** (V / H / IP—$)

We all know how powerful eating dinner together as a family is, and the same is true for your work team. Breaking bread together allows us the opportunity to get to know one another personally. Whether in-person or virtually, have a regular daily lunchtime. Encourage your team to leave their desks and eat lunch together in the lunchroom or, if working remotely, over Zoom at least once a week. Ask each other about your meals and share favorite recipes and family traditions. Try out the Twenty Questions game as a way of getting to know your new teammates a little better. Consider having a monthly or quarterly potluck lunch where your teammates bring their favorite family recipes.

- ***Host a "bring your kids or pets to work" day*** (H / I—$)

  Or if this feels too complicated, share photos and/or stories about kids and pets on a Slack channel. Learning a bit more about everyone's personal lives will help strengthen bonds and trust among your team.

- ***Host a talent show*** (V / H / IP—$)

  Have an annual staff talent show. Get a date booked on the calendar and encourage your staff to sign up to perform. Whether they want to show off their juggling skills—or do a short stand-up comedy set, musical performance, or athletic feat—this is a fun way for a team to get to know more about each other's hobbies and talents.

- ***"What made your week?" or "Good news"*** (V / H / IP—$)

  My friend Robert Glazer shared that at Acceleration Partners they have a "What made your week?" Slack channel dedicated to the sharing of personal highlights from their fully remote team. Teammates share about family, friends, pets, etc., so they all get to know each other a bit more personally. Similarly, at JAM, as part of our daily huddle, which is hosted by a different teammate each day, we always start off with "Good News." Our "huddle host" shares a little bit of personal good news to get us started and then asks if anyone else has something to share. I loved hearing recently that our social media coordinator, Cassidy, had done her first ever stand-up comedy gig, something I didn't know she was pursuing (and now I'm excited to get to see her perform!).

Lunch 'n Learns

- **TED Talk lunches** (V / H / IP—$)

  Have a weekly or monthly TED Talk series in a meeting room or boardroom over lunch. Have your staff sign up to be the moderator. They choose a favorite TED Talk and present it on screen for those in the office or so those working remotely can join by video call. Then the moderator can host discussion and sharing of perspectives from the TED Talk with everyone in attendance.

- **Soapbox sessions** (V / H / IP—$)

  Have a monthly soapbox session, encouraging your team to sign up to do a presentation about something they are passionate about. These sessions allow people to hone their presentation skills, from creating the slides to actually speaking publicly, which not everyone always has an opportunity to do. Further, these sessions let us get to know our team at a deeper level, as we learn about their personal passions and hobbies. In the past we've had some great soapbox sessions on dinosaurs, whales, and the Hubble telescope, to name a few.

- **_Lunch 'n' Learn_** (V / H / IP—$$)

  Bring in an expert (often at no cost) to share helpful informa-
  tion with your team. Consider topics like financial planning,
  parenting, nutrition, etc. Often experts will do these sessions
  for free as it can also be an opportunity for them to find new
  clients. These types of sessions are easily done in-person or
  virtually, so everyone can attend.

- **_Office book club_** (V / H / IP—$$)

  Ask your staff for suggestions of nonfiction books they may
  like to read and discuss as part of the office book club. Then
  keep a list of all their suggestions. We often choose business
  books, biographies, and self-help. Once every two months,
  send a short survey to your entire staff, informing them of
  the date you intend to host the next book club discussion.
  Ask them whether they plan to attend, and if so, have them
  vote by ranking three books from your ongoing list in order
  of preference. In addition to the title of the book, be sure
  to include a link for more information on each one. Once
  you've collected the results, inform your team of the winning selection. From there, encourage them to buy a hard
  copy, ebook, or audio version, and start reading—so they
  can be ready for a fun discussion in a couple months' time.
  Be sure to reimburse your team who attend for the cost of
  the book. Book club can easily be hosted fully in-person, or
  as a hybrid or fully virtual option. Have a moderator lead

the discussion, ensuring that everyone in attendance gets an equal amount of airtime to share their perspectives and biggest learnings from the book. Consider reaching out to the author of the book your team is reading, if you or someone on your team knows them. Depending on the size of your team, they may be willing to join you for ten to twenty minutes of your book club discussion. We've been fortunate to have some incredible authors like Joey Coleman, Todd Herman, Brian Scudamore, and Terry O'Reilly join us for very impactful discussions about their books in the past. Our team has been hosting a bimonthly book club for close to a decade now, and while we always learn a lot from the books we read, the group discussions end up providing us with the best learning. Reading together as a team is a playful way to learn and educate ourselves.

Play Spaces in Your Office

- ***Ping-Pong / pool / foosball tables*** (H / IP—$$)

  If you're going to have fun options like this in your office, make sure they actually get used! Set up a monthly ladder. Play weekly games of "around the world" Ping-Pong with your full team. This is an entertaining way to play with everyone who is in the office on a given day and is guaranteed to get hearts pumping and laughs happening. As the group encircles the table, each player takes a turn hitting the ball, then dropping their paddle and moving counterclockwise around the table. Create your own rules, whether you are instantly out or get three strikes. The remaining two players stand in place and spin after each shot.

- ***Video game console*** (H / IP—$$)

  Get an old-school video game console, so people can take breaks and play a game of Ms. Pac-Man, Space Invaders, or BurgerTime (a favorite of Jen and Kent's in our office). Or perhaps set up an Xbox or PlayStation console on a big screen in a meeting room or lunch area and get some lunchtime or after-work tournaments going.

- ***Puzzles, coloring books, LEGO, and board games*** (H / IP—$)

  Create a quiet space in your office with puzzles, LEGO, and coloring books and perhaps some cards and board games. Encourage your team to use this area when they need a break by themselves, or to grab one or two others to join in some fun. Working on a puzzle with a colleague while chatting personally or discussing a work matter is a great way to build stronger bonds and connections.

Rewards / Loyalty / Celebrations

- **_Incentive trips_** (V / H / IP—$$$)

  Whether your team is working remotely, hybrid, or in-person, you can set lofty goals together for the organization. Create a "stretch target" for your team to work toward and incentivize them with a fun trip to somewhere warm and sunny if they hit the target. Over the years, we have done this many times and celebrated with multiple trips to Jamaica, Mexico, and even Disney World in Florida. The trips are typically three to four days long, and usually involve missing one or two days of work plus a weekend. As an organization grows in size, trips like this can be trickier to plan for, as you may not be able to find part-time staff to fill in—but perhaps departmental trips can happen if they hit certain goals together. Overall, trips and incentives like this really bond a team as they are working together toward a shared goal. And it is on trips like these that silly, fun memories are made, and friendships are incredibly strengthened.

- **_Core value awards_** (V / H / IP—$)

  Consider having a monthly core value award as we do at JAM. Send out a survey to your team for nominees. Ask the value they are nominating their peer for and a short sentence explaining why. Have the CEO or department lead read out the nominations at a monthly all-hands meeting. Not only is this a gift for those receiving the accolades, but it is also a wonderful opportunity for others on the team to show their gratitude for great work being done, which is a gift in and of itself. Consider having a special trophy or Zoom backdrop or some other fun token to celebrate your monthly winners.

- *Shout-outs* (V / H / IP—$)

  If you use an internal chat like Slack or MS Teams, consider having a channel dedicated to shout-outs. Encourage your team (and lead by example) to shout out great work being done on a daily basis by a variety of different teammates. We typically try to tie our shout-outs to a core value, but sometimes it's just a simple public sharing of gratitude for people on your team and great work they are doing. Our shout-out channel gets used daily, and it is another great way for everyone in the organization to hear about great work going on across a variety of departments.

- *Anniversary celebrations* (V / H / IP—$)

  Find reasons to celebrate your team all year long—the more playful the better. Whether it is a birthday, a wedding, a new baby, or a years-of-service anniversary, you can celebrate in your own unique way and have a lot of fun doing it. As an example, when one of our full-time teammates hits the one-year milestone with us, we have a draft ceremony, officially drafting them as "veterans" to the team. As our organization has a big sports focus, we give everyone a hockey jersey with our company logo on the front and their name on the back, along with the number representing the year they started working with us. These vet jerseys typically hang on the wall or on the backs of people's chairs at our head office, or on the walls in people's home offices. The ceremony is casual, yet the recognition is significant and appreciated.

- **Office decor** (H / IP—$)

  Consider getting some fun decor around your office that is in alignment with your purpose and values. Hang photos that commemorate special incentive trips or fun events you've done together as a team. Seeing these pictures on your office wall will incentivize and excite newer teammates to create their own fun memories as a team in the future.

Leadership Opportunities

- **Mayor** (V / H / IP—$)

  My partner Rob got the inspiration to have an office Mayor years ago, after visiting the G Adventures office where he witnessed their Mayoral speeches in action. He loved this playful culture idea so much that we adopted it at JAM. Three times a year we now host a JAM Mayoral Election, such that anyone on the team can run for Mayor, pitching their platform as to how they plan to infuse fun and play into the culture at JAM. The Mayor is provided with a budget for their four-month reign, and it is their responsibility to plan two or three fun socials for the team during that season. After a Mayor's reign, they get a silly photo of them hung on our office wall to commemorate their time as Mayor.

JAM—Mayor wall of fame.

- **Huddle leader** (V / H / IP—$)

  Have a daily huddle—a short meeting that all staff are encouraged to attend as frequently as possible. Ensure important metrics and updates are shared, but sprinkle the meeting with playful segments like "Good News" and "Leader's Choice" as well. The key is ensuring that you have a different huddle leader every day and that all employees are given this opportunity. When hierarchy is removed and everyone in the organization is provided a leadership opportunity, you get to see and know elements of people on your team that you might not otherwise (especially if you don't work with them on a regular basis). And it gives everyone the opportunity to add a little bit of their own playful nature into your culture. As an example, my teammate Marlin from Kalamazoo, Michigan will forever be known as the huddle leader who said "Happy Friday, Junior" one Thursday a couple of years ago—a saying that has since stuck and been said every Thursday huddle since!

Miscellaneous

- **Sports and award show pools** (V / H / IP—$)

  Between the NFL, March Madness, the Olympics, or Stanley Cup, there is always a sporting event for your office team to get excited about. Similarly, whether the Oscars or the Grammys, fun can be had choosing favorites and getting some fun, playful betting going among the team.

- **Field trips or socials** (H / IP—$)

  Encourage your office Mayor to keep their eyes open for different happenings in the cities where your team is working from. Whether your team works remotely or in-person, make plans to gather in person to go on field trips to art galleries, live music, improv shows, or sporting events. Spending time out of the office and getting to know your team personally while enjoying some fun experiences is priceless.

- **_Other random playful ideas for connection_** (V / H / IP—$)

  - Leave your desk and talk to someone, or call them through your team chat and simply get curious and ask them about themselves.

  - Take a stroll and bring someone along, or enjoy a "walk and talk" chat with a teammate on the phone while getting in a short walk. Consider booking walking meetings whenever you don't need to be in front of a computer, and encourage your team to do the same.

  - Spend five minutes with your team answering a fun question of the day.

  - Have impromptu sit-ups, push-ups, or plank challenges with whoever is around.

  - Enjoy a three-minute dance break with your team—turn up the tunes and everyone can get up and dance.

  - Keep some foam balls on hand in the office. In our "homecourt" area where many of our team sits in an open concept way, it can get loud at times. I gave everyone a sports-themed Nerf ball to toss at someone if they were being too loud—a playful way to help everyone focus on the work at hand.

As you can see, there are infinite ways to connect through play in the workplace. For more inspiration and fun resources and ideas to incorporate a little play at work, go to kristiherold.com/resources. Find ways to make it happen, as it pays to play.

"Necessity may be the mother of invention,
but play is certainly the father."

—ROGER VON OECH

ACKNOWLEDGMENTS

I am grateful to have been raised in a family that cherished play. My dad (John Herold) and late mum (Judy Herold) encouraged us to play outside, play sports (any and all we were interested in), play music, play cards and board games, just use our imaginations and *play*. To my brothers, Cameron and Todd Herold, thank you for tolerating my tagging along to play with you and your friends as we were growing up. And Cameron, thank you for inspiring me to put my passion for play into a book that could help inspire others. I am also grateful for my late Grama and Nana, who spent hours playing with me as a little girl. I cherish the memories from many games of pick-up-sticks, Rummoli, and hearts that helped make rainy cottage days pass by quickly.

To my oldest, dearest friends, Judy Gougeon, Mel Duras, Christie Henderson, Trish Magwood, Tori Barton, Sarah Ferguson, Lynnie Bushell, Rebbeca Irwin, Bay Ryley, Dayna

Forsyth: I am grateful for your willingness to play sports, travel, and go along with me and my love of playing pranks over the years. And thank you for your belief in me and your help in spreading the word to encourage so many friends to join the Toronto Central Sport & Social Club (TCSSC) back in the late '90s. I'm so grateful to all the "OG" members of the TCSSC who really got the ball rolling (pun intended) and helped the community to grow to where we are today.

To my many incredible friends, mentors, and fellow entrepreneurs in my Arete forum (Robert Glazer, Jon Levitt, Dennis Blankemeyer, Eric Namaan, Alex Yastrebenetsky, Joey Khatari, and Kuty Shalev), my Six in the 6 forum (Christie, Julie Mitchell, Shelli Baltman, Ann Gomez, and Christine Thomlinson), and of course, from MMT where there are so many special souls (Jayson Gaignard, Adam Franklin, Alon Ozery, Alyssa Kerbel, Barry Glassman, Ben Greenfield, Brad Pedersen, Brad Weimert, Brian Scudamore, Caroline Irving, Chris Ashenden, Chris Taylor, Clay Hebert, Curtis Christopherson, Danny Iny, Dan Jacob, Dan Martell, Darryl Hicks, David Burkus, Dev Basu, Erik Huberman, Gareth Everard, Greg Habstritt, Greg Smith, Jesse Cole, JJ Virgin, Joey Coleman, Jonathan Keyser, John Hall, Jordan Harbinger, Kandis Marie, Kelsey Ramsden, Kieran Matthew, Maria Dakas, Matthew Bertulli, Matthew Christopherson, Michael

Bourbonnais, Mike Desjardins, Michel Falcon, Mike Brcic, Nathan Barry, Nicholas Kusmich, Phil Carvaggio, Philip McKernan, Ray Minato, Renee Warren, Rob Bent, Ronsley Vaz, Saud Juman, Shane Skillen, Sherry Walling, Sol Orwell, Sunny Verma, Todd Herman, Tony Gareri, Tracey Ivanyshyn, Trevor Newell, and Tucker Max). Each of you in these various groups has inspired me as authors and business leaders, and at some point along the way, you have selflessly either shared an idea, an insight, an experience, an introduction, a chat, or been willing to test out our JAM services and/or help spread the word to help us grow. You have each played a role in helping me to grow as a person, as a leader, and to improve my business. The many special people in all of these communities have touched my life in ways that I will be forever grateful for.

To my Bedford Park Players (BPP): you all know who you are. Our years of playing, singing, and dancing together have created some of the strongest bonds of friendship a girl could ask for—thank you. Sarina Condello, I am so grateful that you acquiesced and agreed to work with me to start an adult community musical theater group for charity. The BPP has been a play-filled community where we all have felt vulnerable yet supported, we have shared tears and adventures, and we have laughed harder together than any group of middle-aged amateur thespians I know.

Thank you to Scott Beffort for mentoring me and your support and gentle nudges along the way. And to the many of my friends, teammates, and clients who agreed to be interviewed and share their stories to help bring this book to life, including but not limited to the following: Gerrard Schmid, John Herold, Brian Savage, Sandeep Kembhavi, Taylor Lewis, Barry Glassman, Kara Goldin, Tracey Kasin, James Renwick, Mari Wager, Rob Davies, Levi Cooperman, Bruce Poon Tip, Jonathan Lister, Ray Minato, Marissa Lewis, Tracey Ivanyshyn, Tricia Carrol, Brit Smith, Francine Moore.

To Mark Chait, huge thanks—you were a joy to work with, helping to pull all these stories out of me and create a framework for my ideas. I could not have done this without you. And huge thanks as well to my publishing manager, Katie Villalobos, for helping to oversee and coordinate this entire project. And to the entire team at Scribe, thank you for helping me get a simple idea into an actual book.

To my entire former and current team at JAM (formerly Sport & Social Group), I appreciate the energy each and every one of you has put into helping keep people playing over the last twenty-six years. Further, I appreciate all your help toward crafting our own organizational culture. You have each left your own unique mark on our culture which is engaging, playful, and world-class, in my opinion—a true team effort. While working hard and playing hard ourselves, we have connected millions of people through play, creating a lot of positive ripples around the world. I also want to specifically thank one of our newest teammates, Susan Lute, who helped read and edit this manuscript with insightful feedback, as well as my business partners of over twenty years each, Rob Davies and Rolston Miller—thank you for giving me your blessing to pursue this book project, thank you for all you both do to keep people playing, and thank you both for your thoughtful ideas, suggestions, and edits to the early drafts of this book. I appreciate you all. Let's keep chasing our vision!

Lastly, I have so much gratitude for my family who supported me unconditionally when the pandemic first hit, and it became the most challenging time in my entrepreneurial journey. When I was at my lowest, Cassidy, Andie, Dax, Nicholas, Georgia, Iain, and Dave, you hugged me when I cried, you listened to my crazy ideas, and you encouraged me to never give up. You helped me to believe we would find new ways to keep people playing, and we did!

To my husband Dave, thank you for the multiple read-throughs and the fantastic feedback along the way—this book is better because of you. Thank you also for understanding that one of my love languages is spending quality time together playing—I appreciate having you playing alongside me!

ABOUT THE AUTHOR

An innate entrepreneur, Kristi Herold combined her passion for sport, business, and community in 1996 and founded JAM (formerly Sport & Social Group), one of the largest adult recreational sports league providers in the world, connecting millions of people through play. When the 2020 pandemic forced sports to pause, Kristi's team created a new service: providing professionally hosted virtual (and now in-person and hybrid) events to help corporate teams all over the world stay connected through play.

Kristi has been recognized in the Top 100 Canada's Most Powerful Women and as a top three finalist in the Canadian Women Entrepreneur awards. She has earned multiple Great Places to Work certifications and is a Governor General's "Queen's Diamond Jubilee" recipient.

Made in United States
Orlando, FL
25 April 2024

46178335R00143